MW00814101

Postcard Collector Annual

A Standard Reference For Today's Deltiologist

First Edition
1991
Published by Joe Jones Publishing

Table of Contents

ADVERTISING INDEX

Thank you all!

A special thank you is extended to all the contributing writers featured and to the participating dealers, collectors, suppliers, postcard clubs, and show promoters. Without their loyal support, the *Postcard Collector Annual: A Standard Reference For Today's Deltiologist* would not have been possible. The Staff of *Postcard Collector Magazine*

Advice for the Beginning Collector

By John H. McClintock

With the myriad of postcard topics available on today's market, choosing one or two to collect can be difficult for the beginner.

Animals, Real Photos, Hometown Views, Holidays, Social Issues, War, Artists' Works, etc., etc., etc. The new collector might become confused by the myriad of subjects that appear on postcards. Choosing one or two categories to collect as a starter can be tough!

One need not spend more than they can afford to build an interesting collection and remember, the enjoyment you derive cannot be measured in dollars and cents.

Since we all have different tastes, you alone must decide *what* to collect. It is suggested that you accumulate a variety of cards at first, then take on a couple of subjects. You will find that your favorite subject will change several times in the beginning and that you will branch out into other subjects. For this reason it is best not to insert your beginning collection into albums, as you will be removing them too often.

From a monetary standpoint, there are many subjects that have not yet caught the eye of the investor. Consider topical views of your locality; those "yester-year" records of our recent past can only grow in interest and value. Lesser known artists are still available, and in the comic field, there are many colorful, interesting, and amusing subjects. One can even enjoy collecting the cards of one publisher, whose style may become so familiar to you that you will recognize it without seeing the credits on the address side. Many of the cards are numbered, so you may wish to see how many of them you can locate.

The opportunities for new collectors are better now in these days of awareness than they ever have been, shown by the abundance of postcard publications, lists, auctions, and shows. As the hobby grows and prices of postcards increase, we will see more and more of them come from their long rest in thousands of attics. Most will be preserved in the same condition in which they were lovingly mounted into the albums 50 to 80 years ago.

Always remember that the *quality* of the postcard is important. It is far better to spend a dollar on a card that is in pristine condition than to invest in ten cards that cost ten cents each, but are in poor condition. A used card with the subject or view side in mint condition is just as desirable as an unused card.

Deltiology in the modern sense has advanced in leaps and bounds in the past ten years. Our research and knowledge has only scratched the surface. The next ten years will bring much more prestige and recognition to the fastest growing and wonderful world of postcards. NOW is the time to join in on the fun!

It is suggested that books on postcards be read to give you a feeling for the hobby. Every writer on the subject has a message for you; you will glean a bit of knowledge from each book that will always remain with you. The more you read about a subject, the better you'll understand it. Refer to books often.

Postcard shows can teach the beginner a lot. Check out the exhibits. You will find that they suggest new and varied topics to collect. Visit the dealer tables. You will find that very few of them do not carry the subjects you already collect. Here you can be selective by purchasing the cards in the best condition at competitive prices.

To you, the new collector, the hobby is not simply like opening Pandora's box, it is more likened to jumping into it!

About the Author

Founder and current secretary of the International Federation of Postcard Dealers, John H. McClintock also serves as Director of the Postcard History Society and is a member of 17 postcard clubs nationwide. He also sponsors nine postcard shows annually. Write him at P.O. Box 1765, Manassas, VA 22110.

The "Golden Age" of American Postcards

By George Miller

The concept of a "golden age" can be traced back to Greek and Roman mythology. The phrase refers to an imaginary time in which man was innocent and the world perfect. By extension, it has come to mean a time of great prosperity and achievement—the high water mark.

The "golden age" of postcards in the United States occurred between 1905 and 1915, the decade during which postcards became a national obsession—when Americans bought and mailed postcards by the millions, when publishers competed with one another for the newest and most innovative designs, when entire stores were devoted exclusively to the sale of postcards.

Origins

The idea of a postcard, a small piece of flexible cardboard with a picture or design on one side that was intended to be sent through the mail, was essentially imported from Europe. There were, of course, antecedents in this country that influenced the development of the postcard—illustrated covers, trade cards, advertisements for products and services printed on government postals. Nevertheless, postcards as we know them, were well established in Europe a good 20 years before the craze hit the United States.

The migration had to have been encouraged by several factors. For one thing, the turn of the century brought massive waves of immigrants entering the United States from western Europe. Surely these new citizens were accustomed to buying postcards; they certainly also received a steady flow of postcards from friends and relatives who stayed behind. Moreover, many printers in the United States were German-Americans and, not surprisingly, they were among the first American postcard publishers. Finally, postcards were after all a business—and for a while, a very big business. Eager to create new markets, American businessmen were quick to import what had already proved to be a lucrative business throughout Europe.

The flood of postcards started as a trickle as early as 1898. Until that time, most postcards were printed on the backs of government postal cards. Printers purchased uncut sheets of cards from the U.S. Postal Service, coated and then printed on the backs of the cards, and sold the individual cards. While it was possible to send a private postcard (that is, one not printed on a government postal) through the mail, such cards required two cents postage instead of the one cent on an official card.

In May of 1898, Congress passed the Private Mailing Card Act that established the same postal rate for private cards as for government cards. That Act had the approval and encouragement of the government. The hope was to sell more stamps—it was intended as a revenue-generating measure. The idea worked in a way that exceeded even the most optimistic expectations.

The Flood

By 1905, the *Dry Goods Reporter*, a trade magazine, reported: "The demand for illustrated postal cards is daily assuming larger proportions and there are no prospects of the slightest abatement anywhere in sight." By 1906, postcards were everywhere. *American Magazine* noted: "Bookstores which formerly did a thriving trade in literature are now devoted almost entirely to their sale. There were in Atlantic City last season ten establishments where nothing else was sold, and Chicago, Boston, Pittsburgh, and New York have emporiums where postals constitute the entire stock...These wares may be seen in New York on practically every street corner and most of the drug stores, cigar stands, hotels, barber shops and department stores."

As the decade wore on, the postcard trade penetrated into even the smallest towns in the United States. If no one else in town sold postcards, there was always the local postmaster who generally main-

The Private Mailing Card Act served as a stimulus for the expansion of the postcard publishing industry in the U.S. Among those jumping on the bandwagon was the Hugh C. Leighton Co., Portland, ME.

Children with Postcard Album Bluford, IL

Ambulance Nashua, NH

— I WANT TO BUY REAL PHOTO POSTCARDS —

During the past 15 years, I have been an avid purchaser of **REAL PHOTO POSTCARDS**. I have travelled to numerous shows, bought thousands of cards from dealers and collectors, both here in New England and as far away as California. I would now like to buy many thousands more, hence this advertisement in the *Postcard Collector*. I, too, pay the "going rate." During the many auctions I probably have broken records for the unique **REAL PHOTOS** cards I've purchased. Need I say more?

MAIN STREET REAL PHOTOS - I especially seek active and busy Main Street scenes from any and all U.S. cities and towns. Also store fronts - especially close ups with people and displays. I am looking for store interiors with sharp and detailed features. How about one with the men sitting around a pot-bellied stove? Also want bars, pool rooms, ice cream parlors, barber shops, amusement parlors and theatres. The more striking the image, the more I am willing to pay.

PEOPLE REAL PHOTO - I need thousands of images of people - children and/or adults - even "STUDIO" types especially if unusual (children holding toys, teddies, flags, toy guns etc.) or adults with prominent features (unusual clothing, political, medical problems). Especially want street vendors, occupational, criminals, famous Americans (not mass produced).

COMMERCIAL VEHICLES REAL PHOTO - I love them with vivid, sharp advertising on the side. Both motorized and horse drawn. Send me your remedy wagon (Watkins, Rawleigh). How about delivery wagons with names on the side that match the store behind!

ADVERTISING REAL PHOTOS - automobiles, buses, trucks and all sorts of commercial products where the product is shown in the photo.

SOCIAL HISTORY REAL PHOTO - identified street parades, political (especially socialism), prohibition, women's suffrage, police activity, labor strikes, "Wanted" cards. Also need strikingly patriotic cards especially Uncle Sam or women draped in flags. Also Ku Klux Klan, identified disasters (fires, floods, wrecks) which have a significant photo impact. Also looking for early aviation, western mud street scenes, gambling, Black Americana (especially close-ups), coast to coast walkers, scenes showing early photographers at work, scenes showing postcard production or displays, and identified historic events.

I will buy individual cards or large collections. Send individually priced on approval or for my offer. All real photo cards must be pre-1930 in very fine condition (sharp, clear non-soiled, non-faded images) immediate payment for cards purchased.

LANDMARK POSTCARDS

Bruce Nelson
207-799-7890

P.O. BOX 3565
PORTLAND, ME 04104

House of David Souvenir Makers, showinig dolls Benton Hbr. MI

Watkins Remedy Wagon with Salesman

Postcard shops proliferated during the "Golden Age."

tained several racks of postcards as a side business.

Also involved on the local level across the United States were small town photographers. Unable, of course, to support themselves from studio work alone, they marketed their local photographs on postcards. To aid them, Eastman Kodak by 1902 was producing a postcard-size developing paper on which images could be printed directly from negatives. In 1903, Kodak took the real photo postcard a step further by introducing the first inexpensive camera designed to take postcard-size (3-1/4 by 5-1/2 inch) negatives. Photography, which had originally required the skill of an amateur scientist, was now safely and easily placed into the hands of every person—ironically in the form of the real photo postcard.

The number of postcards sent through the mail during the golden age is staggering. In the first four days of September 1906, 175,000 postcards were mailed from Coney Island. The yearly figures were astronomical. During 1908, almost 670 million postcards passed through the mails. In Baltimore during the 1909 Christmas season, postal employees handled more than a million postcards. By 1913, almost one billion postcards were mailed each year in the United States. Considering that these statistics record only the number of cards mailed, not the total number of cards sold, it is easy to see why the postcard became a big business during that golden decade.

Why?

Why though? What was it about the postcard that gripped the public's imagination? In part, it was a fad. Everyone bought and mailed cards; every family had a postcard album on the table in the parlor. But the popularity of the postcard

was far more complicated than that of the hula hoop or the pet rock.

Postcards were, and still are after all, a means of communication. The majority of cards were bought to be sent to someone else. One of the advantages of corresponding on a postcard was that it simply took fewer words. You didn't have to fill a sheet of paper; a couple of sentences were enough. If there was a pre-printed message, the whole process was even simpler—just sign your name. Even the emphasis on collecting or saving postcards was an outgrowth of this desire to communicate. The family albums so common in the golden age were, for example, typically filled with cards sent from family and friends. Collectors of postcards wanted postally used cards, and they actively exchanged with others bitten by the collecting bug.

Written communication was also

important because the telephone had not yet penetrated into all levels of American society. Local telephone exchanges were often not interconnected; long distance calling was frequently impossible and always expensive. The postcards offered an inexpensive alternative.

The growth of postcards was surely connected, as well, with the development of rural free delivery. Until 1898, home mail delivery was made only in towns with a population of 10,000 or more. This meant that 25 percent of the total population of the United States picked up its mail at the nearest post office. Given the distances involved and the transportation available, for many Americans, mail was a weekly rather than a daily occurrence. By 1906, however, most of the rural delivery routes had been established. Given the new, easy access to regular delivery, it was not surprising that Americans increased their correspondence.

Certainly in part, postcards also represented a way of breaking the geographic isolation in which so many Americans lived. Travel, when it occurred, was by horse and buggy on unpaved roads or by rail. In 1905 there were only about 79,000 automobiles and trucks registered in the entire United States, and paved roads were essentially found only in larger urban areas. If travel was expensive and time consuming, one could "travel" imaginatively through the view card.

Finally, the view card offered something that we today take for granted—a photograph. Prior to 1920, newspapers did not carry photographs, nor did magazines. Living as we do in an age of instant images, it is hard to imagine what it must have been like in 1905, for example, to be able to see and purchase inexpensive photographs of places that you might never be able to visit.

The real photo process put postcard production into the hands of the general public.

The Types

The range of subject matter available on the postcard is unlimited, yet three broad categories contain the overwhelming majority of postcards produced during the golden age—the view, the greeting, and the advertisement.

The view was (and still is) the staple of the postcard industry. While certainly not every building in America in the golden age can be found on a postcard, very few escaped the postcard photographer. If you include real photo cards, probably most towns in America are pictured on dozens, it not hundreds, of different postcards. How different it is today. I cannot buy a single postcard that shows the town in which I live; yet for the period from 1905 to 1915, when Newark, DE, had no paved streets and a population of at best 2,000 people, over 150 different views of the town were produced.

Probably the next largest category for postcards was the greeting card, sent for every holiday from Halloween through Ground Hog's Day, for every occasion from birthdays to wedding anniversaries. The postcard filled the role today played by the folded greeting card. During the period from 1905 until 1915, if you wanted to send a holiday greeting, or to wish someone a happy birthday, or to announce the birth of a child, you sent a postcard. Imagine today, for example, what the postcard industry would be like if there were no folded greeting cards. While it might seem astonishing to think that in, for example, 1910, most American cities with a population over 40,000 had at least one store that specialized in postcards, that probability is not surprising when compared to the greeting card industry. After all, I live in a town of about 40,000 people, and it has five stores that are exclusively devoted to selling folded greeting cards, in addition to a number of others which have at least several racks of cards.

Many businesses made extensive use of the postcard as well. In an age before radio and television, before cheap bulk rate mailings, before billboards (after all there was only an occasional car on those unpaved roads), before extensive advertising campaigns in magazines and newspapers, before even discount coupons, the postcard was an inexpensive and convenient way to reach every American.

The variety of postcards is endless, and that variety is part of the attraction of postcards for most collectors. Think of a subject—any subject—and you will eventually find it on a postcard. Postcards documented every event, no matter how minor. Whenever Americans paraded or celebrated, when buildings burned or rivers

STUDENTS.

Our Parisian Post Card Holder for decorating as shown above will produce a beautiful, artistic effect in your room. Will be sent postage paid on receipt of 25 cts., coin, stamps or money order. Money refunded if not satisfactory.

PARISIAN NOVELTY COMPANY,
757 Broadway, Dept. C, New York.

The demand from collectors for more and more cards not only brought about a variety of topics ranging from state capitols to dressed animals, it also created the need for postcard accessories such as this Parisian Post Card Holder.

flooded, when candidates ran for political office or suffragettes demonstrated, the postcard was there to capture the occasion.

The variety promoted collecting, and collectors in turn stimulated the industry to produce sets and series intended for a collectors' market. Sets of state capitols, state and college girls, homes of the presidents, horoscopes, literary characters, naval vessels, popular songs, famous paintings, religious events—the list is endless. Children were not forgotten—there were sets of bears and babies, dressed animals and days of the week, nursery rhymes and nightly prayers. Soon it was not enough for the cards just to be bright, colorful, and embossed—now they had moving parts; they lit up when held to a lamp; they revealed hidden messages when moved in a certain way or exposed to heat. They were decorated with real feathers, real hair, attachments of every size and shape. They were made of metal, wood, leather, celluloid, and they came in all sizes and shapes.

The Bubble Bursts

At the height of the golden age, many people expected the postcard craze to last indefinitely. But every good businessman knew better. Fads come and go with astonishing rapidity, and the postcard was not immune. By 1912, the industry was cutting back. The change came as the result of a number of factors. Most of the best American postcards were still printed in Europe, and increased tariff rates meant a more expensive retail product. In cost-cutting efforts, many American manufacturers flooded the market with low-cost, low-quality cards. The glut of cards on the market further depressed the industry. One by one, American postcard publishers went out of business. In 1914, the National Association of Post Card Manufacturers canceled their annual convention because of a lack of interest.

As the decade progressed, world conditions also changed. War in Europe also brought the end of the German postcard printing industry. Even if German printers had continued to produce cards, the British blockade of German ports would have prevented their exportation. By the time the U.S. entered the war, anything connected with Germany was suspect.

This is not to say, however, that postcards disappeared. They didn't; they remained an important part of the American stationery market. What changed, though, was the national obsession. No longer were postcards everywhere. No longer did every house have a postcard album in the parlor. No longer were there thousands of collectors eager to purchase the newest designs and novelties. The golden age was over.

About the Author

George Miller has been a regular contributor to Postcard Collector *since its first publication. George attributes his knowledge of postcards to his longevity. Pictured here is George in some of his many manifestations—(figure 1) as the owner of a cigar and tobacco store in Buffalo (his birthplace), (figure 2) as an adopted member of the Ponca Indian tribe in Oklahoma, (figure 3) as a stage star in a British production of* Jack and Jill. *Visitors to the National Postcard Collector Convention in Milwaukee should be aware that this occasion is actually the annual "Miller's Mass Meeting" (figure 4).*

Bitten by the Postcard Bug

By Steven L. Yost

"A postcard show! And you say there's going to be one in Atlanta, November 3rd and 4th. Hmmmm...let me see, what am I doing Saturday? I believe I can get down there by, say, 10:00 and get home by 1:00. Now, how do I break this news to the wife..."

The above was my reaction to a letter I received from Michael Leach of the National Postcard Exchange. Through a book on postcards I found in the local library, *Postcard Companion, The Collector's Reference*, I learned that Atlanta hosts a postcard show every fall. At the time, it was already October, and I figured that the fall show had come and gone. But, what the heck, I thought, I'll send a postcard to the National Postcard Exchange, and if the show's in November, I'll be in luck.

As it turned out, the show was to be held in November. I made my plans to go, described to Debbie, my wife, what I was going to do (as if I knew what to expect), and set out Saturday morning about 9:00 to go to Atlanta. To be honest with you, I really didn't know what to expect. What I found, though, was not what I expected. Reflecting back, I guess I expected large metal racks filled with postcards, postcard posters, and poster postcards. I expected various displays to be set up showing the history of the postcard and even thought that a slide presentation of some early 'Gruss Aus' or 'Tucks' postcards (remember, I checked out the *Postcard Companion*, and I know some of these things now) would be shown. Maybe there would be a seminar on postcard collecting.

The day started out great. There was a cheerful man to greet me at the registration table. I registered, got my door prize ticket (a number written on—what else—a postcard), two postcard collector periodicals, and various other bits of paraphernalia that advertised things like where

and when the next postcard show will be. And then, I walked into the show room.

What I saw wasn't at all what I thought I would. I saw folks sitting at banquet tables that were lined with little boxes, and I mean boxes, of cards laid out in neat little rows. I bet each box held at least a 1,000 cards. There must have been at least 30 different "distributors" there, and each person sat behind, amongst, or within his table configuration. Some of the boxes on the tables were organized by states, some by subject, and most were arranged alphabetically. There were no shiny post-

---

These cards, though once purchased, written, mailed, read, and kept by strangers, were now somehow mine.

---

card racks in sight, no giant poster postcards, no sounds of a slide projector whirring in the corner, and no scheduled seminars or demonstrations in progress, only tables lined with boxes full of postcards. I walked around the place twice, the second time just to make sure I didn't miss something on the first go-round.

"Now what am I going to do?" I asked myself. Then, I thought "what was that man's name who replied to my request for information on the fall postcard show? His letter is back in the car. I better go and get it." So, back to the car I went to get Michael's name. "No big deal," I said to myself, "this will give me a chance to get rid of all this stuff I picked up at the registration table, and I can go back in with my hands free (I did pocket the door prize postcard; after all, maybe they will call out #85)."

Returning from the car, I went back inside, found Michael, and introduced myself to him. He remembered who I was and asked me if there was anything in particular that I was looking for that he could help me find. I didn't want to say that I was just browsing, so I asked him where the movie poster postcards were that National advertised in the literature that he sent me. He showed me the box of movie postcards, and I sifted through the box of cards for about 15 minutes (more on how I sifted later, but for you who are in the business; I'm sure you can guess my procedure).

I found a movie poster postcard and for 50 cents I was off to circle the place again. Michael thanked me for stopping by and bid me farewell. I'm sure he wished that I would have found more than one card and spent more than 50 cents. I really wasn't interested in movie poster postcards. I thought that if I had found a Marilyn Monroe movie poster postcard, I would have gotten it for Debbie; she likes Monroe items.

I was now wandering aimlessly around the place. It was at this point that I began to study the group. There were possibly 50 of us customers in the room. While the other 49 were intently sorting through handfuls of cards at a time, very carefully and meticulously, I was watching them. "What are they looking for?" I asked myself. "Surely they are not looking for a card that they remember their Aunt Millie may have sent them back in the '50s." Some of the people even brought in notebooks—notebooks that were already filled with postcards. I guess this was for them to compare their cards with the ones that were on sale or possibly to keep them from buying duplicate cards.

After some more trips around the room, I finally noticed the marker system of sorting through cards. One of the dealers had placed a sign up indicating what a marker was and how it was to be used. The sign read something like this: "Please don't sift through our cards; use a marker and sort through our cards a few at a time." I was about to leave and call the trip a total disaster when suddenly, out of the blue, I found myself looking at a box of Florida cards.

The Florida box was indexed by cities, and St. Petersburg was one of the cities tabbed. "Well, what do you know, postcards from old St. Pete," I said to myself as I started looking through them (using the marker system, of course). What I found were old, but in good condition, postcards of the beach I used to know and still love on Treasure Island. My grandparents lived on Treasure Island when I was a kid, and now my mom and dad live there.

When we lived in Tampa, we used to go to the beach almost every weekend during the summer. I found postcards of St. Pete and Treasure Island that really took me back to my youth. These were places I knew and could remember. "This is great, I'll buy this one, and this one, and this one, too."

My prize catch of the day were the postcards of Webb's City. If you're not familiar with St. Petersburg and Webb's City, Webb's City was (it no longer is) a building that took up an entire city block.

It was touted as the world's most unusual drug store.

Webb's City had mermaids, and within the boxes of postcards I even found one featuring these maidens of the sea. You see, there was a section of the store that looked liked a rock cave. Portholes were provided in the rock walls to see into the cave. Inside, there was a shipwreck scene with mermaids lounging about. These were special mermaids...they talked to you. Somehow, they knew your name and could see that you had just gotten a haircut or that you had come back to see them again. It was an unbelievable corner of the store and *the* place to be and see when you were five years old. It didn't matter that the card was $3.00. I had to have it.

All of a sudden, I was having fun. I now had a mission, and there were 30 dealers to visit. "Where are your Florida cards?" I would ask. "You mean, your cards aren't alphabetized, categorized, or indexed by city and state. Maybe I'll be back later!"

I ended up buying 20 old postcards. I even won a $5.00 door prize, which I used to buy some of these cards. Most of the postcards had been through the mail, and I got to eavesdrop on what people wrote to their friends and relatives back home. I plan to frame or somehow display

these cards in my home soon. These cards, though once purchased, written, mailed, read, and kept by strangers were now somehow mine. They held memories temporarily forgotten with the passage of time.

So, for me, the postcard show turned into a giant surprising and successful venture. In one sense, the show did not meet my expectations; however, in another sense the show surpassed my expectations.

As I close this article, I am reminded of the words to the song that Bob Hope always sings at the end of his shows: "Thanks for the memories." And to this I would like to add, "let's make some new memories next time!" See you at the next show and, maybe by then there will be a seminar planned on postcard collecting.

About the Author

New to the world of postcard collecting, Steven L. Yost, Acworth, GA, will surely be attending more postcard shows in the future, now that he's been "bitten by the bug." For a list of postcard events, check out the show calendar in this edition of the Postcard Collector Annual.

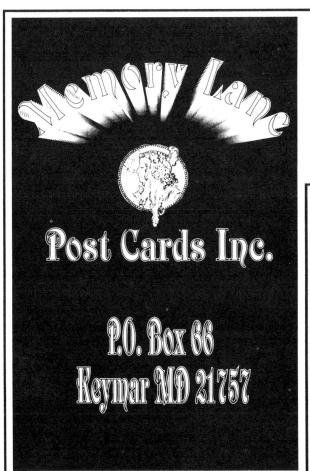

Show Calendar

This show calendar listing is provided to help postcard collectors find dealers offering postcards at shows in their area. To have your show listed in the 1992 *Postcard Collector Annual*, mail the information, using the form on page 77, to *Postcard Collector Annual*, P.O. Box 337, 121 North Main Street, Iola, WI 54945 before March 1, 1992.

APRIL

Apr 5-6 WI, Milwaukee. 2nd Annual National Postcard Collector Convention. MECCA Convention Center, 500 W. Kilbourn Ave. 10am-8pm, A: $3.50/day, $5.00/show, free to *PC* subsc. *Postcard Collector* Magazine, P.O. Box 337, Iola, WI 54945. PH: 715-445-5000.

Apr 5-6 NJ, Mt. Laurel. POCAX '91. Budget Motor Lodge, Exit 4, NJ Tnpk (adjacent to Trailways Bus Station). Fri. 10am-8pm, Sat. 10am-5pm, A: $1.50. 25 dealers. South Jersey Postcard Club, Carlton Bloodgood, P.O. Box 111, Bogota, NJ 07603.

Apr 5-7 ENGLAND, Guildford. South of England International Postcard Show. Civic Hall, 30 mi. from London. Fri. 11:30am-9pm, Sat. 10am-7pm, Sun. 10am-5pm. 80 PC dealers. Roy Allen, 14, Wheatlands, Hounslow, London, England, TW5 0SA. PH: 081 570 7458.

Apr 6 NY, Oneida. Central New York Postcard Club Show. St. Paul's United Methodist Church, Sayles St. (off Rt. 5). 9am-4pm, A: $1.00. 15 PC dealers. Ruth R. Weimer, RD 2, Box 173, Rte. 31, Canastota, NY 13032.

Apr 6 OH, Springfield. Postcard & Paper Show. Clark County Fairgrounds, I-70 exit 59. 9am-5pm, A: $1.50. Ron Hilbert, Box 67, Unionville Center, OH 43077. PH: 614-873-4552.

Apr 6-7 CA, Santa Cruz. 5th California Central Coast Post Card & Paper Memorabilia Show. Holiday Inn, 611 Ocean. Sat. 10am-6pm, Sun. 10am-4pm, A: $1.00. Phyllis Annet, 1100 Vailwood Way, San Mateo, CA 94403. PH: 415-345-6211 eve.

Apr 6-7 WA, Bellingham. Bellingham Stamp, Coin & Postcard Show. Lakeway Best Western Inn, 714 Lakeway (exit 253 off I-5). Sat. 10am-6pm, Sun. 10am-4pm, A: free. Tripo Costello, 1030 16th St., Bellingham, WA 98225. PH: 206-733-5309.

Apr 7 IL, Collinsville. 2nd Spring Metro-East Postcard Show. VFW Hall, 1234 Vandalia (Hwy 159). 9am-6pm, A: free. Holger (Danny) Danielsen, P.O. Box 630, O'Fallon, IL 62269. PH: 618-632-1921.

Apr 7 NY, Levittown, Long Island. Long Island Post Card Club's 14th Postcard & Ephemera Show. YOM Center, Center Lane. 10am-5pm, A: $2.00. PH: 516-754-1214.

Apr 7 NY, Lockport. Lockport Coin & Stamp Club's 28th Coin, Stamp & Post Card Show. Best Western Lockport Inn, 515 S. Transit (Rt. 78). 10am-5pm, A: free. 5 PC dealers. Norman A. Trimmer, 6452 Hatter Rd., Newfane, NY 14108.

Apr 13-14 VA, Manassas. Postcard Society Show. Ramada Inn, Rt. 234 at I-66. Sat. 10am-7pm, Sun. 10am-4pm, A: free. John McClintock, Box 1765, Manassas, VA 22110.

Apr 13-14 IN, Evansville. Twin Bridges 4th Annual Postcard & Paper Show. Robert E. Green Convention Center, Room Indiana A, 600 Walnut St. Sat. 8:30am-10am (members), 10am-6pm (public), Sun. 10am-4pm, A: free. 20+ PC dealers. Mike Finley, RR1, Box 847, Tell City, IN 47586. PH: 812-836-2747. Sarah Cooper, 3307 W. Maryland St., Evansville, IN 47720. PH: 812-424-7866.

Apr 14 CT, Meriden. 10th Annual Connecticut Postcard Club Show. Ramada Inn, 275 Research Pkwy (I-91 East Main St. exit). 8:30am-10am (members only), 10am-5pm. 30+ PC dealers. Peter Maronn, 180 Goodwin St., Bristol, CT 06010. PH: 203-589-6984.

Apr 20 NY, Albany. Upstate New York Regional Ephemera Fair. Thruway House, 1375 Washington Ave. 10am-5pm, A: $3.50. 35 PC dealers. Oliver & Gannon Associates, P.O. Box 131, Altamont, NY 12009. PH: 518-861-5062.

Apr 20-21 CA, San Diego. Greater San Diego Postcard & Paper Collectibles Show. Scottish Rite Temple, 1895 Camino Del Rio S., Mission Valley. Sat. 10am-7pm, Sun. 10am-4pm. Nick Farago, P.O. Box 217, Temple City, CA 91780. PH: 818-287-6066.

Apr 20-21 IN, Indianapolis (Carmel). Indianapolis Postcard Show. Keystone Square Mall, 116th St. & Keystone. Sat. 10am-10pm, Sun. 12noon-5pm, A: free. 25 PC dealers. Robert Pickard, 5010 W. 22nd St., Indianapolis, IN 46224. PH: 317-241-8777.

Apr 20-21 PA, New Stanton. 10th Ohio Valley Regional Antique Picture Postcard Show. Knights Court Convention Center, PA tnpk. exit 8. Sat. 10am-6pm, Sun. 10am-5pm, A: $1.00. 15 PC dealers. Mary Martin, American Historic Postcard Society, 231 Rock Ridge Rd., Millersville, MD 21108. PH: 301-987-7550.

Apr 21 MA, Watertown. Bay State Post Card Collectors' Club Show. Armenian Education & Cultural Center, 47 Nichols Ave. 9am-4pm, A: free. 40 dealer tables. William S. Crane, 898 Mass. Ave., Apt. 6, Arlington, MA 02174. PH: 617-646-3576.

Apr 21 IL, Rockford. Rock Valley Postcard Club Show. Forest Hills Lodge, Rt. 173 (next to Rockford Speedway). 9am-5pm, A: free. 30 PC dealers. George W. Gibson, 405 W. Hurlbut, Belvidere, IL 61008. PH: 815-547-8558.

Apr 27 MI, Kalamazoo. Southwest Michigan Post Card Club's 8th Post Card Bourse. Kalamazoo County Fairgrounds, 2900 Lake St. 9am-4pm, A: free. Sue Hodapp, 1415 Seminole, Kalamazoo, MI 49007. PH: 616-344-2545.

Apr 28 WI, Milwaukee. Milwaukee Postcard Show & Sale. Gonzaga Hall, 1441 S. 92nd St. 10am-5pm, A: $1.00. 30 PC dealers. Frank Greiczek, 3041 N. Humboldt Blvd., Milwaukee, WI 53212. PH: 414-264-0225.

Apr 28 NY, Stamford. 13th Annual Post Card Show. V.F.W. Post, Rt. 10 (3/4 mi. beyond Red Carpet). 10am-5pm. 25 tables. Carlton & Dorothy Bloodgood, 211 Oakwood Ave., Bogota, NJ 07603.

MAY

May 2-8 MA, Brimfield. Hopkins "Start of the Mart." 9am-9pm. 15+ PC & paper dealers. Jose Rodriguez, P.O. Box 903, Cheshire, CT 06410. PH: 203-272-2841.

May 3-4 OH, Olmsted Falls. Western Reserve Postcard Society, Leanu Park, 7370 Columbia Rd. (Rt. 252 south of I-480). Fri. 11am-7pm, Sat. 10am-5pm, A: $1.00. 36 PC dealers. Paul Knapp, 25028 Rainbow Dr., Olmsted Falls, OH 44138. PH: 216-234-4441.

May 11 WV, Clarksburg. West Virginia Postcard, Stamp & Paper Show. Holiday Inn Bridgeport, I-79 & U.S. 50. 9am-5pm, A: $1.00. 7 PC dealers. Edward Roth, P.O. Box 4252, Parkersburg, WV 26104. PH: 304-679-5609.

May 17-18 IL, Hillside. Windy City Postcard Show. Hillside Holiday Inn, I-290 & Hwy 45. 10am-9pm. Susan Nicholson, P.O. Box 595, Lisle, IL 60532. PH: 708-964-5240.

May 17-18 PA, York. Ye Olde York Show. York Mall, 2801 E. Market St. 10am-9pm, A: free. 28 PC dealers. Corinne Rodermond, 3111 Eastern Blvd., York, PA 17402. PH: 717-755-8035. Jerry Kotek, 424 Corbin Dr., York, PA 17403. PH: 717-843-3479.

May 17-19 NY, New York. 14th International Post Card Bourse. Days Inn, 440 W. 57th St. Fri. 11am-7pm, Sat. 10am-7pm, Sun. 11am-5pm, A: $3.00, $5.00/2 days, $7.00/3 days. Leah Schnall, 67-00 192nd St., Flushing, NY 11365. PH: 718-454-1272 or 0582.

May 19 FL, Palm Beach Gardens. Palm Beach Stamp, Coin & Baseball Card Festival. Holiday Inn, PGA Blvd./I-95. 10am-5pm, A: free. 5 PC tables. Joseph Banfi, P.O. Box 1198, Stuart, FL 34995. PH: 407-283-2128.

May 19 ME, Portland. Pinetree Postcard Club's Annual Spring Show. Italian Heritage Center, 40 Westland Ave. (behind Shaw's Westgate Shopping Center). A: $1.00. Pinetree PC Club, P.O. Box 6815, Portland, ME 04101.

May 19 MT, Helena. Montana Postcard, Baseball Card, Book & Paper Show. Colonial Inn Ballroom, 2301 Colonial Dr. 10am-5pm, A: $1.00. 6-8 PC dealers. Tom Mulvaney, P.O. Box 814, E. Helena, MT 59635. PH: 406-227-8790 after 8pm.

May 19 IA, Cedar Rapids. Cedar Rapids Post Card Club Show. Sheraton Inn, 525 33rd Ave. SW. 9am-5pm, A: free. Vivian Rinaberger, 4548 Fairlane Dr. NE, Cedar Rapids, IA 52402. PH: 319-393-6743.

May 24-25 MD, Hagerstown. Postcard Society Show. Howard Johnson Hotel, 107 Underpass Way (exit #5 off I-81). Fri. 10am-7pm, Sat. 10am-4pm, A: free. John McClintock, Box 1765, Manassas, VA 22110.

May 25-26 KS, Merriam (Kansas City). Heart of America Postcard Collectors, Inc. Annual Show. Merriam Community Center, 5701 Merriam Dr. (Johnson Dr. exit off I-35, two blocks west, three blocks north). Sat. 9am-5pm, Sun. 9am-4pm. Don Harmon, 12806 W. 71st St., Shawnee, KS 66216. PH: 913-268-6149.

JUNE

Jun 1 NY, Slate Hill. 12th Annual Half Moon Postcard Club, Inc., Show. Minisink Valley High School, Rt. 6 (10 min. west of Middletown). 9am-5pm, A: $1.00. 40 PC dealers. Dee Dee Backus, 636 Greenville Tpk., Port Jervis, NY 12771. PH: 914-856-3461.

Jun 2 PA, Shamokin Dam. 7th Annual Susquehanna Valley Post Card Club Postcard Show. Holiday Inn, Rts. 11 & 15 (across bridge from Sunbury, PA). 9am-5pm, A: $1.00. 24 PC dealers. Joe Epler, P.O Box 132, Northumberland, PA 17857-0132. PH: 717-473-3466

Jun 2 NY, Oswego. Post Card Club of Oswego County Postcard Show & Sale. Scriba Fire Hall, two miles east from Oswego on Rte. 104 (Bridge St.). 10am-5pm, A: $1.00. Lillian M. McCloskey, 7 W. 8th St., Oswego, NY 13126. PH: 315-343-1049.

Jun 2 OH, Columbus. Columbus Paper Fair. Veterans Memorial Convention Center, West Hall, 300 W. Broad St. 9am-5pm, A: $2.50. Columbus Productions, Inc., 3280 Riverside Dr., Suite 18, Columbus, OH 43221. PH: 614-459-7469.

Jun 7-9 CA, Pasadena. Greater L.A. Postcard & Paper Collectibles Show. Elks Hall, 400 W. Colorado Blvd. (corner of Orange Grove & Colorado). Fri. 1pm-8pm (earlybird 11am-1pm), Sat. 10am-6pm, Sun. 10am-4pm, A: $3.50 per day or $5.00 for show. Nick Farago, P.O. Box 217, Temple City, CA 91780. PH: 818-281-3390.

Jun 8-9 CA, Pasadena. Nostalgia & Collectibles Show & Sale. Pasadena Exhibit Center, 300 E. Green St. Sat. 11am-6pm, Sun. 11am-4pm, A: $5.00. 20 PC tables. Doug Wright, P.O. Box 69308, West Hollywood, CA 90069. PH: 213-656-1266.

Jun 8-9 MA, Farmington. Farmington Antiques Show. Farmington Polo Grounds. Sat. 7am-6pm, Sun. 9am-4pm, A: $3.00, early bird $20.00. 10 PC dealers. Abby McInnis, P.O. Box 388, Grafton, MA 01519. PH: 508-839-9735.

Jun 9 OH, Cincinnati. 7th Annual Cincinnati Postcard Show. Ramada Hotel, 5901 Pfeiffer Rd. & I-71 (exit 15). 9am-5pm, A: $2.00. Don Skillman, 6646 Shiloh Rd., Goshen, OH 45122. PH: 513-625-9518.

Jun 9 BC (Canada), Vancouver. 4th Annual Vancouver Post Card Club Show & Sale. Hastings Community Center, 3096 E. Hastings St. 8am-4pm. Lance Arnett, 2260 King Albert Ave., Coquitlam, BC V3J 1Z5. PH: 604-931-6146. D. Steele, 1840 Orchard Way, West Vancouver, BC V7V 4G2. PH: 604-922-9688.

Jun 14-15 NY, Corning. Corning National Antique Postcard Fair. Corning Glass Center Auditorium. 9am-5pm. Mary Martin, American Historic Postcard Society, 231 Rock Ridge Rd., Millersville, MD 21108. PH: 301-987-7550.

Jun 15 OH, Ashland. Johnny Appleseed Postcard Club's 13th Annual Show. Ashland High School, corner of Katherine Ave. & King Rd. off S.R. 42. 8am-4:30pm, A: $1.00. 30 PC dealers. James R. Perkins, P.O. Box 132, Ashland, OH 44805.

Jun 16 NH, Hudson. 8th Annual Granite State Post Card Collectors Club Spring Show & Sale. Hudson Lions Club Hall, off Rt. 111 to Adelaide St. to Lions Ave. 9am-3pm, A: $1.00. 40 PC dealers. Edith Costa. PH: 603-428-3752.

Jun 21-22 PA, King of Prussia. Postcard Society Show. Geo. Washington Lodge, Rt. 202 & Warner Rd. Fri. 10am-7pm, Sat. 10am-4pm, A: free. John McClintock, Box 1765, Manassas, VA 22110.

Jun 21-22 IN, Elkhart. Giant Collectible Show. Concord Mall, US 33 East. A: free. Gene F. Haberstich, P.O. Box 908, Goshen, IN 46526. PH: 219-533-1887.

Jun 29-30 WA, Kent. Greater Seattle Postcard & Paper Collectibles Show. Kent Commons, 425 4th Ave. W. Sat. 10am-6pm, Sun. 10am-4pm, A: $3.00. Nick Farago, P.O. Box 217, Temple City, CA 91780. PH: 818-287-6066.

JULY

Jul 6 OH, Columbus. Heart of Ohio Post Card Club's Summer Show. Quality Inn, E. Broad St. & Hamilton Rd. 10am-4pm A: $1.50. Ron Hilbert, P.O. Box 67, Unionville Center, OH 43077. PH: 614-873-4552.

Jul 7 ME, Saco. Pinetree Postcard Club's Annual Saco Postcard Show. Saco Elks, Rt. #1 (across from Funtown USA). Pinetree Postcard Club, P.O. Box 6815, Portland, ME 04101

Jul 12-13 PA, York. First Annual Show of York Postcard Club. Bridgeton Center at Howard Johnson's Motor Lodge, Rts. 30 & 83. Fri. 12noon-8pm, Sat. 9am-5pm, A: $1.00. 24 PC dealers. Jerry Kotek, 424 Corbin Rd., York, PA 17403. PH: 717-843-3479.

Jul 13-14 CA, San Francisco. San Francisco Postcard Sale. Sheraton Airport Hotel, Hwy 101, Broadway exit. Sat. 10am-6pm, Sun. 10am-5pm, A: $3.50, $3.00/ad. Jan Banneck, P.O. Box 26, San Ramon, CA 94583. PH: 415-837-7907.

Jul 20 ME, Portland. Maine Paper Americana Show. Portland Exposition Building, 239 Park Ave. 10am-5pm, A: $3.50. 70 PC dealers. Oliver & Gannon Associates, P.O. Box 131, Altamont, NY 12009. PH: 518-861-5062.

Jul 20-21 CO, Denver. Colorado Classic Post Card Show. Continental Hotel, exit 212-B west from I-25. Sat. 10am-6pm, Sun. 10am-4pm, A: $1.00. 25 PC dealers. Giorgian Zekay, Denver Post Card Club, 3033 Valmont, Sp. 31, Boulder, CO 80301. PH: 303-442-2469, mornings.

AUGUST

Aug 16-17 IN, South Bend. Midwest Postcard Exposition. Century Center, Downtown South Bend. Fri. 10am-6pm, Sat. 9am-5pm, A: $1.50. 35 PC dealers. Tom & Alice Zollinger, 1023 Markle Ave., Elkhart, IN 46517. PH: 219-522-3954.

Aug 18 ME, Portland. Grab Bag Antiques, Inc. Postcard Show. Verrillos Convention Center, 155 Riverside St. (exit 8 off ME Pike). 10am-5pm, A: $1.50. 35 PC dealers. Alan Grab, P.O. Box 630, Sabattus, ME 04280.

Aug 24-25 IL, Collinsville. Gateway Postcard Club 16th Annual Show. Collinsville Gateway Convention Center, One Gateway Dr. (off Hwy 157). Sat. 10am-6pm, Sun. 9am-4pm, A: Sat. $1.00, Sun. free. Danny Danielsen, P.O. Box 630, O'Fallon, IL 62269. PH: 618-632-1921.

Aug 30-31 KY, Louisville. Postcard Society Show. Hurstbourne Hotel, I-64 & Bluegrass Pkwy. Fri. 10am-7pm, Sat. 10am-4pm, A: $1.00. John McClintock, Box 1765, Manassas, VA 22110.

Aug 31-Sep 1 MA, Farmington. Farmington Antiques Show. Farmington Polo Grounds. Sat. 7am-6pm, Sun. 9am-4pm, A: $3.00, early bird $20.00. 10 PC dealers. Abby McInnis, P.O. Box 388, Grafton, MA 01519. PH: 508-839-9735.

SEPTEMBER

Sep 14-15 CA, Arcadia. San Gabriel Valley Postcard & Paper Collectibles Show. Arcadia Masonic Temple, 50 West Duarte Rd. Sat. 10am-6pm, Sun. 10am-4pm, A: $3.00. Nick Farago, P.O. Box 217, Temple City, CA 91780. PH: 818-281-3390.

Sep 15 MT, Helena. Montana Postcard, Baseball Card, Book & Paper Show. Colonial Inn Ballroom, 2301 Colonial Dr. 10am-5pm, A: $1.00. 6-8 PC dealers. Tom Mulvaney, P.O. Box 814, E. Helena, MT 59635. PH: 406-227-8790 after 8pm.

Sep 21-22 CA, Glendale. Great Collectibles Show & Sale. Glendale Civic Auditorium, 1401 N. Verdugo Rd. Sat. 11am-6pm, Sun. 11am-4pm, A: $5.00. 20 PC tables. Doug Wright, P.O. Box 69308, West Hollywood, CA 90069. PH: 213-656-1266.

Sep 27-28 OH, Columbus. 16th Annual Heart of Ohio Post Card Show. Aladdin Temple, 3850 Stelzer Rd. (I-270, Morse Rd. exit). Fri. 9am-6pm, Sat. 9am-4pm, A: $1.50. Betty Sidle, 444 Heather Ln., Powell, OH 43065. PH: 614-548-5265.

Sep 28 IA, Clive (Des Moines). Hawkeye Postcard & Paper Show. 11001 University Ave. 9am-5pm, A: free. 17 PC dealers. Agnes J. Aller. PH: 515-279-5418.

Sep 28 MA, Dennis. Cape Cod Postcard Collectors

Club 6th Annual Show & Sale. Dennis Senior Citizen Center, Rt. 134 (exit 9 off Mid-Cape Hwy, Rt. 6, left 2 mi.). 9:30 am-4:30 pm, A: $1.00. 32 PC dealers. Hugh Daugherty, P.O. Box 1146, Eastham, MA 02642 (send SASE). PH: 508-255-7488.

Sep 28-29 VA, Manassas. Postcard Society Show. Ramada Inn, Rt. 234 at I-66. Sat. 10am-7pm, Sun. 10am-4pm, A: free. John McClintock, Box 1765, Manassas, VA 22110.

OCTOBER

Oct 5 CT, Manchester. Greater Hartford Postcard Show & Sale. East Catholic High School, Exit 60 off I-84. 9am-4pm, A: $2.50. 30 PC dealers. Herb Stevenson, P.O. Box 333, Manchester, CT 06040. PH: 203-649-7560.

Oct 5 IN, Indianapolis. First Hoosier Postcard Show. Downtown Convention Center, 100 S. Capitol Ave. (next to Hoosierdome). 9am-5pm, A: $2.00. George Mitchell, 2154 N. Talbott, Indianapolis, IN 46202. PH: 317-924-0712.

Oct 12 IL, Homewood. Homewood-Flossmoor Postcard Club's 13th Annual Post Card Show & Bourse. Dolphin Lake Clubhouse, 183rd St. & Governors Hwy. 10am-5pm, A: free. Les Lawitz, 18820 Highland Ave., Homewood, IL 60430. PH: 708-957-0874.

Oct 12-13 OR, Portland. Greater Portland Postcard & Paper Collectibles Show. Scottish Rite Temple of Portland, 709 S.W. 15th St. (corner of 15th & Morrison). Sat. 10am-6pm, Sun. 10am-4pm, A: Sat. $3.00, Sun. $2.00, Webfooter's free. Nick Farago, P.O. Box 217, Temple City, CA 91780. PH: 818-287-6066.

Oct 12-13 NJ, Somerville. 32nd Annual Postcard Show of the Garden State Post Card Collectors Club. 4-H Center, Milltown Rd. (off Rt. 202, 2.5 mi. S. of traffic circle). Sat. 10am-7pm, Sun. 10am-5pm, A: $1.00. 40+ PC dealers. Dolores Kirchgessner, 421 Washington St., Hoboken, NJ 07030. PH: 201-659-1922.

Oct 12-13 IN, Elkhart. Giant Collectible Show. Concord Mall, US 33 East. A: free. Gene F. Haberstich, P.O. Box 908, Goshen, IN 46526. PH: 219-533-1887.

Oct 13 IA, Cedar Rapids. Cedar Rapids Post Card Club Show. Sheraton Inn, 525 33rd Ave. SW. 9am-5pm, A: free. Vivian Rinaberger, 4548 Fairlane Dr. NE, Cedar Rapids, IA 52402. PH: 319-393-6743.

Oct 19 MI, Kalamazoo. Southwest Michigan Post Card Club's Post Card Bourse. Kalamazoo County Fairgrounds, 2900 Lake St. 9am-4pm, A: free. Sue Hodapp, 1415 Seminole, Kalamazoo, MI 49007. PH: 616-344-2545.

Oct 19-20 KS, Wichita. 14th Annual Wichita Postcard Club's Show. Wichita Postcard Club, P.O. Box 780282, Wichita, KS 67278-0282. PH: 316-686-5574.

Oct 20 NY, Newark. 16th Annual Western New York Post Card Club Show & Sale. Quality Inn-Newark (formerly Sheraton-Newark Inn), 125 N. Main St. (Rt. 88). 9am-4pm, A: $1.00. Edward J. Beiderbecke, P.O. Box 155, Williamson, NY 14589. PH: 315-589-2287.

Oct 25-26 MD, Timonium (Baltimore). PIKPOST '91. Days Hotel Timonium, 9615 Deereco Rd. (I-83 at exit 17, Padonia Rd.). Fri. 10am-7pm, Sat. 10am-4pm, A: $1.00. 25 PC dealers. Perry Judelson, Box 7675 Baltimore, MD 21207. PH: 301-655-5239 (eve).

Oct 27 WI, Milwaukee. Milwaukee Postcard Show & Sale. Gonzaga Hall, 1441 S. 92nd St. 10am-5pm, A: $1.00. 30 PC dealers. Frank Greiczek, 3041 N. Humboldt Blvd., Milwaukee, WI 53212. PH: 414-264-0225.

NOVEMBER

Nov 1-2 VA, Ashland. 14th Annual Old Dominion Postcard Club Show. Best Western Motel, Atlee' Elmont exit off I-95. Fri. 10am-7pm, Sat. 10am-4pm, A: $1.00. John McClintock. PH: 703-368-2757.

Nov 2 NJ, Belmar. Jersey Shore 7th Fall Postcard Show. On the Boardwalk, Ocean Ave. (between 5th & 6th Aves.). 9am-4pm, A: free. John McGrath, 95 Newbury Rd., Howell, NJ 07731. PH: 201-363-3121 evenings.

Nov 8-10 NY, New York. Metropolitan Post Card Club's Post Card Show. Days Inn, 440 W. 57th St. Fri. 11am-7pm, Sat. 10am-7pm, Sun. 11am-5pm, A: $3.00, $5.00/2days, $7.00/3days. Leah Schnall, 67-00 192nd St., Flushing, NY 11365. PH: 718-454-1272 or 0582.

Nov 9-10 IL, Bloomington. Cornpex '91. Scottish Rite Temple, near intersection of Rt. 51 N. & Rt. 9 E. Sat. 10am-6pm, Sun. 10am-4pm, A: free. 15 PC dealers. Janice Jenkins, Box 625, Bloomington, IL 61702-0625. PH: 309-663-2761.

Nov 22-23 PA, York. York International Antique Postcard Fair. York Fairgrounds, exit on Rt. 30 from I-83. Fri. 9am-7pm, Sat. 9am-5pm. Mary Martin, American Historic Postcard Society, Inc., 231 Rock Ridge Rd., Millersville, MD 21108. PH: 301-987-7550.

DECEMBER

Dec 6-7 PA, New Stanton. 10th Ohio Valley Regional Antique Picture Postcard Show. Knights Court Convention Center, PA tnpk. exit 8. Sat. 10am-6pm, Sun. 10am-5pm, A: $1.00. 15 PC dealers. Mary Martin, American Historic Postcard Society, 231 Rock Ridge Rd., Millersville, MD 21108. PH: 301-987-7550.

Dec 6-7 NJ, Mt. Laurel. Postcard Society Show. Budget Motor Lodge, Rt. #73 (exit #4 off NJ tnpk). Fri. 10am-7pm, Sat. 10am-4pm, A: free. John McClintock, Box 1765, Manassas, VA 22110.

Dec 7-8 CA, San Diego. Greater San Diego Postcard & Paper Collectibles Show. Al Bahr Temple, 5440 Kearny Mesa Rd. (at Frwy. 163). Sat. 10am-7pm, Sun. 10am-4pm, A: $3.50. Nick Farago, P.O. Box 217, Temple City, CA 91780. PH: 818-287-6066.

1992
JANUARY

Jan 11-12 WA, Kent. Greater Seattle Postcard & Paper Collectibles Show. Kent Commons, 425 4th Ave. W. Sat. 10am-6pm, Sun. 10am-4pm, A: $3.00. Nick Farago, P.O. Box 217, Temple City, CA 91780. PH: 818-287-6066.

Jan 18-19 CA, Sacramento. 6th Annual California Capital Show. Scottish Rite Temple, 6151 H St. Sat. 10am-6pm, Sun. 10am-4pm. Rudy & Natalie Schafer, 2820 Echo Way, Sacramento, CA 95821. PH: 916-971-1953.

FEBRUARY

Feb 8-9 CA, San Francisco. San Francisco Postcard Sale. Sheraton Airport Hotel, Hwy 101, Broadway exit. Sat. 10am-6pm, Sun. 10am-5pm, A: $3.50, $3.00/ad. Jan Banneck, P.O. Box 26, San Ramon, CA 94583. PH: 415-837-7907.

MAY

May 17 IA, Cedar Rapids. Cedar Rapids Post Card Club Show. Sheraton Inn, 525 33rd Ave. SW. 9am-5pm, A: free. Vivian Rinaberger, 4548 Fairlane Dr. NE, Cedar Rapids, IA 52402. PH: 319-393-6743.

May 22-23 WI, Milwaukee. 3rd Annual National Postcard Collector Convention. MECCA Convention Center, 500 W. Kilbourn Ave. 10am-8pm, A: $3.50/ day, $5.00/show, free to PC subsc. Postcard Collector Magazine, P.O. Box 337, Iola, WI 54945. PH: 715-445-5000.

JUNE

Jun 13-14 MA, Farmington. Farmington Antiques Show. Farmington Polo Grounds. Sat. 7am-6pm, Sun. 9am-4pm, A: $3.00, early bird $20.00. 10 PC dealers. Abby McInnis, P.O. Box 388, Grafton, MA 01519. PH: 508-839-9735.

JULY

Jul 11-12 CA, San Francisco. San Francisco Postcard Sale. Sheraton Airport Hotel, Hwy 101, Broadway exit. Sat. 10am-6pm, Sun. 10am-5pm, A: $3.50, $3.00/ad. Jan Banneck, P.O. Box 26, San Ramon, CA 94583. PH: 415-837-7907.

SEPTEMBER

Sep 5-6 MA, Farmington. Farmington Antiques Show. Farmington Polo Grounds. Sat. 7am-6pm, Sun. 9am-4pm, A: $3.00, early bird $20.00. 10 PC dealers. Abby McInnis, P.O. Box 388, Grafton, MA 01519. PH: 508-839-9735.

OCTOBER

Oct 11 IA, Cedar Rapids. Cedar Rapids Post Card Club Show. Sheraton Inn, 525 33rd Ave. SW. 9am-5pm, A: free. Vivian Rinaberger, 4548 Fairlane Dr. NE, Cedar Rapids, IA 52402. PH: 319-393-6743.

Keeping Your Postcards Alive

By Katherine Hamilton-Smith

Postcards are more fragile than you might think. They should be handled and stored carefully to ensure their long-term survival in both private and institutional collections.

The paper on which postcards are printed is made of plant fibers. High in cellulose, plant fibers also contain starches, sugars, carbohydrates, and the organic acid lignin. For hundreds of years, paper was made by hand from cotton or linen rags; a process accomplished without additives, which would have had a deteriorative effect on the finished product. As literacy increased, so did the demand for paper and the need for larger sources of plant fibers to produce it. Increased mechanization in the production of paper produced more paper faster, but reduced quality. Earlier printed books, such as a Gutenberg Bible, are still in wonderful condition today; the paper still pliable and white. Books produced since the late 18th century are typically yellowed and brittle by comparison. Some estimates indicate that up to 40 percent of the books in libraries in the United States will soon be too fragile to be handled and used by patrons. This dismal scenario is not exemplified only by our libraries. It extends much further to almost all common papers produced in the last 150 years, including postcards and other paper ephemera.

The trouble is easily traceable. Common paper made since circa 1850 was produced with groundwood (wood pulp) as the source of cellulose and sized with alum-rosin (a double sulfate of aluminum which degrades to sulfuric acid). The combination of wood pulp as the basic plant fiber and its impure components of alum and lignin gave the paper a high acid content. And acid is the main culprit in the destruction of paper. Staining, brittleness (i.e. paper which breaks after one or two folds), and weakness in a paper object, whether it is a page in a book or a postcard, is caused by the breakdown of the molecular structure of the cellulose in paper. The rapid yellowing of newspaper, which is made of wood pulp produced quickly and impurely and is consequently very acidic, provides a good visual example of this breakdown. The paper used to produce postcards is not typically of a high quality either. The ephemeral nature of postcards meant that they were not produced with materials intended to last. Great care must be exercised in order to preserve them, as they are already in a state of rapid destruction. Acidity is measured on the pH scale of 0 to 14. A reading of pH7 is neutral and readings above pH7 are basic; as the reading decrease toward 0, the acidity increases. The pH reading for postcards printed by the Curt Teich Company, for example, is about 4.5, which is very acidic.

Sound complicated? Yes and no. In practical usage, you can do some very simple things to substantially increase the life of your collection. It is worth the time to consider your own collection and how it is stored. It is vitally important with real photo postcards that whatever enclosures you use be made of materials which *will not react* with the chemistry of the photography. Remember that any paper product, such as file folders, boxes, envelopes, mounting board, or mats which come into contact with postcards should be "acid free" and "lignin free" and have

> **Although it is slow, the damage taking place in your collection, even as you read this article, is usually *irreversible*.**

an alkaline buffer added to create a pH of 8.5. However, with certain types of photographic processes (albumen, dye transfer, cyanotype, and chromogenic prints) buffered sleeves are *not* recommended. Many postcard collectors store their collections in shoe boxes or shoe box-sized cardboard containers. Unless you *know* that your boxes are made of acid free materials, they are probably giving off acidic gases and peroxides in substantial quantities which will have damaging effects on your postcards over time. If the containers you use have lids, this only increases the damaging effects, because the destructive gases from both the box container itself and the postcards stored within are transmitted through the air as well as by physical contact.

Plastic sleeves are commonly used by postcard collectors to store and display their collections. Be aware that not all of the plastic products available for such purposes are safe in terms of preserving paper. One plastic which is often used to make photographic album pages and display sleeves is polyvinyl chloride (PVC). This plastic degrades easily and quickly and emits gases and plastic by-products which are extremely harmful to paper objects and photographic emulsions. Some PVC products actually become sticky when they degrade; a stickiness which could permanently harm anything stored inside a PVC sleeve. Plastics which are safe for storing postcards are polypropylene, cellulose triacetate, polyester, and polyethylene. These plastics are inert or chemically stable and have a neutral pH, and therefore will not degrade in the presence of fluctuating temperature, humidity, light levels, or when in contact with acidic materials. Of these four plastics, polyester is the most inert and most rigid. Archival polyester may already be familiar to collectors under its marketing names of DuPont's Mylar D

and ICI's Melinex #516. For long-term storage of real photo postcards, paper sleeves would be preferable, but for collectors who wish to look at items in their collections often, polyester sleeves (or an archival equivalent) would be the best choice, as it would reduce the need for constant removal and replacement of postcards from their storage sleeves.

For a private collector or dealer, the single most important tip about the care of your collection is careful handling. This is especially crucial with real photo postcards. The front or image side of a real photo card is actually the emulsion side of a photographic print and as such is extremely fragile. Finger oils, scratches, dust, and to a certain degree, environmental conditions can be kept from damaging photographs by always placing them in protective archival sleeves. Not only does this protect the postcard somewhat from potentially damaging handling, it also serves as a psychological barrier between the postcard and anyone handling it. A sleeve silently says that you care about the postcard and that you are taking measures to protect it. So often, collectors are seen at bourses rapidly thumbing through stacks of postcards. Flipping through a huge stack of postcards in this way shows little regard for each individual card as a fragile object worthy of preservation. The only advantage to this is speed. But the flipping motion will quickly abrade the edges of the cards, making them soft and weak. Go slower. Take more care. Never lick fingers in order to give them more flipping power. Wash hands frequently, especially after touching food of drink.

Deterioration of paper and photographs is often imperceptibly slow. On a day to day basis you cannot see the subtle

Figure 1: Postcard showing damage from label taped to front. Photo courtesy Lake County Museum, Curt Teich Postcard Archives, Wauconda, IL.

changes which indicate that an object is falling apart. Because the damage is so subtle, it can, in the words of photographic conservator James Reilly, director of the Image Permanence Institute in Rochester, NY, "foster a stubborn inertia about initiating preservation practices." To help get started, perhaps it would be useful to remember that although it is slow, the damage taking place in your collection, even as you read this article, is usually *irreversible*. Especially with photographic materials, once damage has occurred through careless handling, stor-

age in acidic containers, or some more dramatic and sudden event such as water or adhesive coming into contact with the postcard, it can *hardly ever* be returned to its original condition. Whatever you do or cause to happen to items in your collections while they are in your care, is probably permanent.

A Few Dos and Don'ts

•Never use paper clips, rubber bands, any kind of adhesive or pressure-sensitive tape to secure stacks of postcards. Tape, adhesive, and rubber bands will all degrade very quickly and leave permanent marks (figures 1 and 2). And as they degrade, their chemical breakdown may react with photographic chemistry. Paper clips tend to rust and leave indentation marks.
•Never use ink *of any kind*, even on the backs of postcards. Modern felt tip pens are especially notorious for degrading quickly and "soaking" completely through a paper object to the opposite side from the original marking. Only pencil is appropriate for marking on paper or photographic materials. Never mark on the front or image side of a photographic.
•Never use any sleeve or other enclosure made of polyvinyl chloride (PVC). Always use inert plastics.
•Never use any kind of paper (especially "kraft" paper), cardboard, mat board, or boxes made of materials which are acidic or contain lignin. Common shoe boxes or corrugated boxes are especially bad.
•Never use envelopes which are con-

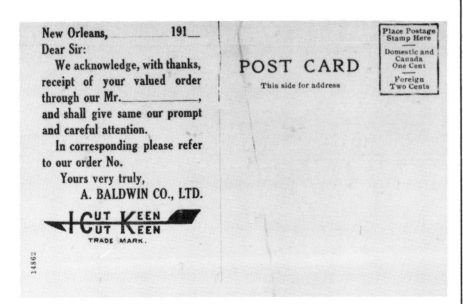

Figure 2: 1912 postcard back showing mark from rubber band. Photo courtesy Lake County Museum, Curt Teich Postcard Archives, Wauconda, IL.

structed with a center seam. These seams are usually glued together with unstable adhesives which will migrate to objects stored within, staining or otherwise damaging them.

•Keep collections away from direct light, both natural and artificial.

•The ideal temperature for storage is 65 degrees F and 50% relative humidity (RH), kept at a constant level year-round. But this is difficult if not impossible to maintain in a home situation. The best place to store collections in domestic structures which have no environmental regulation is in an interior closet (not against an exterior wall). Closets are dark and tend to have the least extreme fluctuations of temperature and RH. Do not keep collections in basements or attics; these two locations rival each others as the *worst* places in any house in terms of extremes of temperature and RH.

•Never file postcards away with newspaper clippings.

•Try to avoid human oil and perspiration coming into contact with postcards, *especially* photographic postcards. If, for some reason, you cannot sleeve individual cards, make a concerted effort to handle them respectfully, holding them by their edges and never putting your fingers on the face of the cards.

Suppliers

It is easy to find the archival materials you need to properly care for your postcards. The following list of suppliers is recommended by museum conservators and curators. Most of the catalogs from these companies are free of charge and have useful information about the care of paper and photographs, in addition to ordering information. In the last few years, several of the companies have added materials specifically developed for postcard storage and care.

•The Hollinger Corporation, 3810 South Four Mile Run Drive, P.O. Box 6185, Arlington, VA 22206. 800-634-0491.

•University Products, 517 Main Street, P.O. Box 101, Holyoke, MA 01041. 800-628-1912.

•Conservation Resources International, 8000-H Forbes Place, Springfield, VA 22151. 800-634-6932.

•Light Impressions Corporation, 439 Monroe Avenue, P.O. Box 940, Rochester, NY 14603. 800-828-6216.

For Further Reading

•Lener, Dewayne J. *Paper Preservation: Conservation Techniques & Technology.* Heritage Quest Press, Orting, WA. 1988.

•Reilly, James M. *Care & Identification of 19th Century Photographic Prints.* Eastman Kodak Company, Rochester, NY. 1988.

•Ritzenthaler, Mary Lynn, Gerald Munoff and Margery S. Long. *Archives & Manuscripts: Administration of Photographic Collections.* Society of American Archivists, Chicago. 1984.

•Ritzenthaler, Mary Lynn. *Archives & Manuscripts: Conservation.* Society of American Archivists, Chicago. 1983.

•S.D. Warren Company. *Paper Permanence: Preserving the Written Word.* Boston, MA. 1983.

About the Author

Katherine Hamilton-Smith is the Curt Teich Postcard Archives Curator at the Lake County Museum. This article only breaks the surface of the issues related to the proper care of collections. For additional information or clarification of anything in this article, contact the author at the Lake County Museum, Curt Teich Postcard Archives, Lakewood Forest Preserve, Wauconda, IL 60084. PH: 708-526-8638, Monday through Friday 9:00 a.m. to 4:30 p.m. CST. More in-depth information about conservation of paper and photography is easily accessible.

Postcard Supplies Directory

Artwork courtesy Bill Cole Enterprises, Inc.

This listing provides company names, contact names, addresses, and telephone numbers for firms offering display, storage, and preservation supplies for postcards. Directly following this company listing is an alphabetical product listing.

COMPANY LISTING

Abraham's Corner, Bill Cloran, 2708 "Y" St., Lincoln, NE 68503. PH: 402-474-2696.

Ball, Harold J., 2826 S. Harrison St., Fort Wayne, IN 46307.

Bill Cole Enterprises, Inc., P.O. Box 60, Randolph, MA 02368-0060. PH: 617-986-2653. FAX: 617-986-2656.

Blackstamps, Paul Brenner, P.O. Box 402, South Orange, NJ 07079. PH: 201-761-0341.

Buttons By Wilson, Gregory Wilson, 215 Chestnut St., Florence, MA 01060. PH: 413-586-8554.

Dr. Nostalgia, Dr. & Mrs. Bob Gardner, 3237 Downing Dr., Lynchburg, VA 24503.

Hobby House Distributing, Michael Fallon, P.O. Box 2207, Richmond, IN 47375. PH: 317-966-6939 (info), 800-544-6229 (orders).

Majorstamps, Thomas M. Major, P.O. Box 808, Columbus, OH 43216-0808. PH: 614-228-1853.

March Enterprises, Dwight M. March, 2551 Lombardy Lane, Suite 220, Dallas, TX 75220. PH: 214-358-1153.

Mary L. Martin, Ltd., Mary L. Martin, 231 Rock Ridge Rd., Millersville, MD 21108. PH: 800-899-9887, 301-987-7550.

Norton, Russell, P.O. Box 1070, New Haven, CT 06504. PH: 203-562-7800.

Pack & Wrap, 466 Derby Ave., West Haven, CT 06516. PH: 800-541-9782.

Pike's Pricing, John L. Pike, 328 Garfield St., York, PA 17404. PH: 717-845-4710.

Richard Novick Products (Card-Gard), Richard Novick, 17 Abbey Lane, Marlboro, NJ 07746. PH: 908-536-2532.

Shiloh Postcards, Vickie Leach Prater, P.O. Box 2004, Main St., Clayton, GA 30525. PH: 404-782-4100.

The Bag Man, Steve O'Conor, P.O Box 129, Vernon, NJ 07462-0129. PH: 201-764-3535.

20th Century Plastics, 3628 Crenshaw Blvd., Los Angeles, CA 90016. PH: 800-767-0777.

PRODUCT LISTING

ALBUMS
Continental-size
　March Enterprises
　Mary L. Martin, Ltd.
　Richard Novick Products
　20th Century Products
Standard-size
　March Enterprises

　Mary L. Martin, Ltd.
　Richard Novick Products
　20th Century Products
ALBUM PAGES
Archival-quality material composition
　Abraham's Corner
PolyDeluxe (standard)
　Shiloh Postcards
Polyester (Mylar)
　March Enterprises
　Pike's Pricing
Polyethylene
　March Enterprises
　Mary L. Martin, Ltd.
PolyLight (continental)
　Shiloh Postcards
Polypropylene
　Abraham's Corner
　Hobby House Distributing
Polyvinyl Chloride
　Richard Novick Products
Rigid Vinyl
　20th Century Plastics
ARCHIVAL REPAIR MATERIALS
　Bill Cole Enterprises, Inc.
　March Enterprises
BOXES
Archival-quality material composition
　Bill Cole Enterprises, Inc.
　March Enterprises
　Richard Novick Products
Continental-size
　Bill Cole Enterprises, Inc.
　Blackstamps
　Majorstamps
　March Enterprises
　Mary L. Martin, Ltd.
　Pike's Pricing
　Richard Novick Products
Corrugated
　Pack & Wrap
Standard-size
　Bill Cole Enterprises, Inc.
　Blackstamps
　Majorstamps

　March Enterprises
　Mary L. Martin, Ltd.
　Pike's Pricing
　Richard Novick Products
　Shiloh Postcards
BUTTONS
　Buttons By Wilson
CATALOG
　Ball, Harold J.
　Bill Cole Enterprises, Inc.
　Blackstamps
　March Enterprises
　Pike's Pricing
　Richard Novick Products
　Shiloh Postcards
DIVIDERS
　March Enterprises
　Mary L. Martin, Ltd.
　Pike's Pricing
　Shiloh Postcards
ENVELOPES/MAILERS
　Pack & Wrap
　The Bag Man
FRAMES/PLAQUES
　March Enterprises
　Shiloh Postcards
GLOVES
　March Enterprises
MATS
　Buttons By Wilson
MOUNTING CORNERS
　Shiloh Postcards
POLY BAGS
　Pack & Wrap
PRICING LABELS
　Pike's Pricing
　Shiloh Postcards
RIBBONS/SHOW SUPPLIES
　Buttons By Wilson
SLEEVES
　Dr. Nostalgia
Polyester (Mylar)
　Ball, Harold J.
　Bill Cole Enterprises, Inc.
　March Enterprises
　Norton, Russell
　Pike's Pricing
Polyethylene
　Hobby House Distributing
　Majorstamps
　March Enterprises
　Mary L. Martin, Ltd.
　Pike's Pricing
　Richard Novick Products
　Shiloh Postcards
　The Bag Man
Polypropylene
　Ball, Harold J.
　Norton, Russell

The Whys and Whats of Collecting Linens

By Don Preziosi

For five years (1984 through 1988), I wrote a column for *Postcard Collector* that was primarily about linen postcards. By 1984 there was enough general interest in linen postcards for a national postcard magazine to justify a monthly column, but a mere five or six years prior to that the idea would have been inconceivable. In the mid-1970s very few postcard collectors were actively seeking linen cards. Most postcard dealers considered them to be only worthy of their bargain boxes, if that. A few dealers may have had a "motel" category or a "large letter" section, but no one had any category whatsoever that was defined by the word "linens." Time after time the typical responses to my wife's and my requests for linens were "Whaddaya want that junk for?", "I don't carry linens.", or "I throw that stuff out!"—all said with a tone of disgust. We did not give up, because almost every dealer had some linens scattered throughout their stock, and the prices were usually low. Ten cents was the most typical price, though often you could find them for less than a nickel, particularly at flea markets. In our first year of collecting, 25 cents was the most we were willing to pay for superb examples, though as competition increased we raised our limits in the next two years to 50 cents and a dollar.

My, how times have changed! (Such a cliche, but so appropriate.) In 1991, if you go to any large postcard show, you will find that many, if not most of the dealers will have one or more categories that are devoted to linen or Linen Era (1930-1955) cards. Amongst the dealers that have established a clientele for linens, superb examples in certain categories may be priced at $20 or more. Some linens have even changed hands in excess of $100!

Those who don't already collect linen cards might ask if this is a fad. After all, those who have been in this hobby long enough have seen many types, categories, or artists go in and out of fashion with collectors, in spite of the overall upward trend of our hobby through the last two decades. Certainly, extraordinarily high prices might be considered a fluke, but I would have to say that the interest in better linen cards (and consequently prices) has increased steadily, and at times dramatically, in the 14 years that I have been collecting.

Why Linens?

Linen cards were introduced around 1930, primarily because of a new genera-tion of high-speed printing equipment. The linen-textured paper enabled the inks to be absorbed faster. Curt Teich developed this new, color postcard process to revitalize the postcard business at the onset of the Depression. Many other publishers duplicated this system with their own ink variations, but few were able to equal the quality of the Curt Teich firm.

The new, brighter colors, and the regular use of retouching to remove undesirable features (wires, poles, awkward shadows, etc.) and add new elements (beautiful clouds, a moon, extra lights or cars, etc.) made these cards an idealized vision of a growing America. I also think the textured paper added to the effect of making the cards seem like miniature realist paintings. The linen postcard was extremely successful, and Curt Teich became the giant of the American postcard industry. Linen cards dominated the postcard market for almost 25 years.

Now, some of these cards are already 60 years old, and in the great scheme of collecting there is only a 20 or 30 year difference between most lines and an early 1900's "Golden Age" card. Add to this the fact that collectors under the age

 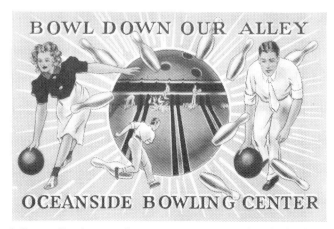

This seemingly larger-than-life sandwich and a transparent bowling ball revealing human pin setters are two examples of why linen advertising cards are hot topics for today's collectors, plus the bowling card has a double appeal for sports enthusiasts.

of, say 50, often find collectibles of the 1930s and '40s more interesting than those of the first couple of decades of this century, and it's easy to come to the conclusion that the demand for Linen Era cards can only increase in the coming years.

In spite of the rise in prices, there are still plenty of opportunities to collect linen postcards without putting a major dent in your finances. Countless postcard collectors have just as much fun collecting 25-cent cards as those that collect 25-dollar cards. The thrill of the hunt is most of the fun for many people, and if you have the stamina and the patience, you can find some cards for a fraction of the price they would sell for at the major east or west coast shows. While some outstanding cards are apparent to any experienced dealer, and therefore difficult to find at a bargain price, certain categories can yield good results, particularly if the dealer whose cards you are looking at does not seem to distinguish between the aesthetic merits of, say, one restaurant card and the next; or is not familiar with availability or rarity of cards in that category.

Topics

There are probably as many different topics covered on Linen Era postcards as on earlier postcards—different topics, of course, but still a wide variety. Providing the topic that one collects is not specific to a certain time frame, there may very well be linen cards that can enhance a collection. The hottest topics have been, and continue to be, "Roadside" and "Advertising." These categories can, and often do, overlap. I use the term "roadside" to encompass a broad range of topics generally associated with automobile travel, but no automobiles per se. Cards advertising specific models of cars would more

Although Gamler's Jewelers and Opticians is the primary focus on this advertising card, Bulova Watches is touted as well.

correctly be included under "advertising" or "transportation."

Other major topics that are available on linens include transportation, military, expositions, pin-ups (the "glamour" cards of the period), comics, sports, animals, and large letters (the "Greetings from _____" cards that are almost synonymous with linen postcards).

Advertising postcards from any era usually have a strong following amongst collectors. Many earlier advertising cards were issued by manufacturers as a sort of souvenir or premium and were thus meant to be collected and saved. Most linen advertising postcards were, however, literally junk mail. They most certainly were not issued to be collected, and they were usually filed not in an album or shoe box, but in the garbage. Thus, those local

advertising linens for a camera shop or shoe store may be extremely rare, even though thousands of each card were printed.

The poster-style cards advertising a product are the most desirable. They are difficult to find and, not surprisingly, the most expensive category of linens. Their graphics can be striking and often have an art deco appearance. Because most were thrown away, many of those surviving are salesmen's samples.

"Roadside" includes motels; hotels; tourist courts, cabins, lodges, and cottages; restaurants, cafes, diners, grills, cafeterias, and drive-ins; theaters; gas stations and garages; car dealers; trailer parks; roadside attractions; billboards; etc. And if I left anything out, I think you get picture. These, too, were free postcards given out at the various gas, food, and lodging establishments. (If you want to get a good idea of some of the wonderful cards in this category, get a copy of John Baeder's *Gas, Food, and Lodging,* published by Abbeville.) Frequently the management of the largest establishments would even pay the postage if you filled out the card and gave it back to them. (Penny postage made it a cheap way to advertise.) Unlike the advertising cards that came directly to your home or place of business, these cards were often saved as mementos of a vacation or trip.

This topic has been consistently popular with collectors for the last 10 to 12 years. As mom-and-pop motels have given way to national chains, and drive-ins, diners, and local eateries have been replaced by fast-food franchises, the nostalgic appeal of these cards only increases. Some of these cards are absolutely awful, and some are quite spectacular. The main difference in collecting these cards now

As fast-food restaurants continue to take over the eatery market, the nostalgic appeal of diner cards only increases.

versus 10 years ago (aside from price) is that 10 years ago those looking for this type of card wanted only better examples. Now, even awful ones have a potential market, and for good reason, not simply because it's harder to find better examples! Enter the view card collector.

Perhaps the biggest change during the last decade in the collecting of Linen Era postcards is that many local view card collectors now seek cards from the '30s, '40s, and '50s to round out their collections. Long ignored by view card collectors for being too new, too garish, or too irrelevant for historical purposes, roadside cards in addition to linen view cards are now recognized by many collectors as being significant additions to the history of any area. And what's more, many of these cards are scarce—far scarcer than a 1910 street scene might be. Even though some of these cards were printed by the thousands (Curteich's most popular linen process, C.T. Art-Colortone, required minimum runs of 6,500 cards), they were not saved in the way that earlier view cards were. This is even more true of local cards that advertised businesses other than those associated with food or lodging.

The Linen Era was an exciting time for U.S. **transportation**. The tremendous increase in auto and bus travel, the burgeoning commercial aviation industry, and the streamlining of the railroads are all well documented on postcards. Railroads companies, airlines, bus companies, and shipping concerns all gave away postcards to passengers. Auto dealers also sent cards of both new and used offerings to prospective customers. (Surprisingly few auto advertising cards are true linens, though the artwork and colors used give them a similar appeal.)

34-05 45th STREET, LONG ISLAND CITY, N. Y. • Tel. RAvenswood 8-3330

As motorized travel increased during the Linen Era, so did the appearance of transportation postcards documenting that increase.

Comics are probably the most underrated category of linen cards. There are many hidden treasures, often at bargain-basement prices. Linen comics spoof everything, including money, food, social mores, sex, military life, work, and leisure time. It is true that some were vulgar, racist, or sexist, but that just makes them a populist reflection of some of the prevailing attitudes of the day. Other topical collectors should take note of comics, because within this category are cards relating to various sports, activities, and vocations.

Many comics were published in sets and series (particularly those of the Curt Teich Company) and that adds to the collecting challenge. Curt Teich published scores of sets, but about a dozen or so stand out because of their highly stylized, art deco-influenced art work.

The **pin-up** cards of the period are sometimes related to the comic cards in that often they were designed to be more humorous than titillating. Although sold individually, they were usually issued as parts of sets or in a numerical series. Bathing beauty cards were usually of photographic origin, but the others were most often of "artistic" derivation.

Since World War II was the major event of the linen era, and linen postcard production was at its peak in the 1940s, there are many collecting opportunities related to the **military**. For all those men and women in U.S. camps, the postcard was an easy way to communicate with the folks back home. It was also cheap because Uncle Sam provided free postage!

All branches of the service and most camp activities were covered. There are a great many sets and series (including comics). Also, there are some interesting propaganda cards. Some were meant to inspire, such as a "Victory" or "Keep 'em Flying" set; others knocked Hitler, the Japanese, or all three Axis leaders.

The most sought after linen cards pertaining to **sports** are major and minor league baseball stadiums. Some are as common as houseflies, and others are scarcer than hen's teeth. Only an experienced eye can separate the fool's gold from the real thing.

Also available on linens are golf courses and country clubs, football stadiums, tennis courts, horse and dog racing, roller rinks and bowling alleys, skiing, skating, and more.

The two major expositions of the Linen Era were the 1933-34 Century of Progress and the 1939-40 New York World's Fair. Both of these were extensively covered on linens, with many different sets and se-

This comic linen makes light of a serious military situation during World War II.

ries, some comics, and some excellent advertising postcards. Other fairs and expos on linens include the Golden Gate Exposition, the Texas Centennial, and the Mardi Gras. Interest in the expos of the period tend to be regional, with East Coast collectors looking for the New York fair, Midwest collectors concentrating on Chicago.

The last category that I'll highlight is the only linen category that has been actively collected since the cards were

produced. These are the **large letter** cards that consist of the name of a city, state, region, or attraction where each letter of the name encloses a different scene. Thousands of different ones were produced, and because they were made in such large quantities, they are still inexpensive to collect—often 50 cents a card or less. There are many clever and/or scarce ones which command a premium.

What Makes a Linen Outstanding?

An outstanding card is, quite literally, a card that stands out. It has stopping power. It commands a second or third look (even if you don't collect that category). Three major criteria contribute to an outstanding card: subject matter, graphics (the design of the card or the visual representation of the subject matter), and print quality. There are also minor factors such as captions, titles, slogans, and design techniques.

The subject matter of the card need not be unusual for the card to be outstanding, and conversely, unusual subject matter does not guarantee an outstanding card.

The list of unusual subjects on linen cards in endless! How about real fish drinking a can of beer, a woman in a dress made of cigars, a gas station in the shape of a mammy, waitresses dressed as lobsters, or a transparent hen, to name a few? However, ordinary subjects can make outstanding postcards simply because they are rarely found on linen cards—a platter of food, a car wash, or Santa Claus.

How a subject is depicted is often

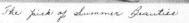

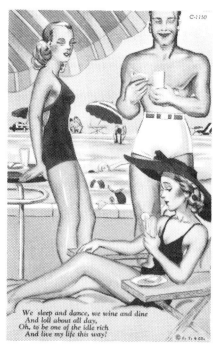

Any of these lovely ladies would have made great pin-ups during the Linen Era. The card at left advertises Airmaid Hosiery, while the other two are from sets—C.T. Bathing Girls (center) and C.T. Fresh Air Comics (right).

more important than the subject itself. A low, wide-angled perspective of a streamlined locomotive gives it the illusion of power and speed that would be lacking in an ordinary shot. A colossal statue of Paul Bunyan is much more interesting (and humorous) with a mere six-foot mortal standing next to Bunyan's boot. A motel card that includes insets of one or two interior scenes reveals a lot more of the atmosphere.

Unfortunately many postcard photographers then, like many amateur photographers today, put too great a distance between camera and subject. This can make even an outstanding subject ineffective. A building shaped like a shoe is not so outlandish when it occupies only five percent of the card.

Few linens show an extreme close-up of anything. Consequently, cards showing a close-up of a person or animal are almost always outstanding because of the novelty of the perspective.

Linens have long suffered from a reputation of being cheaply printed. I certainly would not dare to compare them with the finer printing techniques of earlier cards, but I do believe that the better examples of linens possess a unique beauty. The combination of artistic airbrushing of the original black-and-white photo and the adept application and choice of colors

The only linens to be actively collected since they were produced, large letter cards consist of different scenes from an area enclosed in letters that spell the name of the state, city, region, or attraction.

during the printing process often created a pleasantly fantasized image. Most well-produced linens have this delightful quality.

Some cards may not make it on subject or graphics alone, but have a caption, title, or slogan that is irresistible. How about "When your spirit lags, take a swig at Swags." Or, "Pork from pigs that made hogs of themselves." Or, "St. Jude, patron of hopeless cases, pray for us."

Elaborate borders, unusual typefaces, symbols, silhouettes, and decorations can all enhance a card when used artistically. Ironically, if used to excess, they can overpower the subject and create a card

that is so garish that it becomes collectible for that reason alone!

The important thing to keep in mind when you're collecting linens or any type of cards is to have fun and use them as the springboard for further education and research, be it local history or something whimsical. Collect what interests you, not what necessarily interests everyone else. Read books, ask questions, share your collection with anyone who might be interested. That is the most fun of all. Postcards collectors and dealers are generally a friendly bunch and will probably tell you more than you ever wanted to know, should you ask!

About the Author

Don Preziosi (P.O. Box 498, Mendham, NJ 07945) has been buying, selling, and collecting postcards for 14 years. He and his wife, Newly, have been full-time postcard dealers for over 11 years. Prior to his career in postcards, Don was an advertising art director for 11 years. He has used his experiences from both careers to design, produce, and distribute a contemporary line of postcards on social and political issues. He lives in Mendham with Newly and their two children, Nick and Susanna.

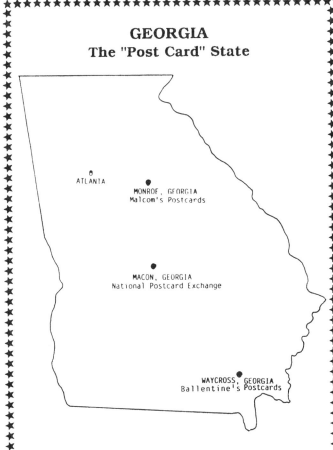

Enjoy A Subscription to

BARR'S  NEWS
Weekly

Enjoy the World's Largest
(and WEEKLY) Deltiology Newspaper

Picture Post Card Collecting is becoming one of the Largest and Most Popular Hobbies in the World.

Post Card Collecting is an Exciting, Affordable Antique!
Post Card Collecting offers a Wide Range of Topics available for collecting!
Post Card Topics parallel and relate to every other collecting interest!

Join the Thousands of Collectors currently interested in U.S. and
World History through the Wonderful Hobby of Deltiology!

Barr's Post Card News, published weekly, can bring you all the
Post Card Events and Shows, News and Articles, Post Card
Club Activities, Current going prices of Post Cards,
Want and For Sale advertising, and Much, Much More!

The Best Of The Post Card World
Barr's Post Card News
Only $25. 00 per year (52 exciting issues)
Canada $35.00 in U.S. Funds. Foreign $150.00 in U.S. Funds.

• •

Subscription Form
Please begin my_____year subscription immediately!

Name _____
Please Print or Type
Address _____
City _____ State _____ Zip _____
Visa/MC # _____ Expiration Date_____

For bigger savings, consider our multiple year subscription discounts:
2-Years: $46.00 • 3-Years: $66.00 • 5-Years: $105.00

Barr's Post Card News
70 S. Sixth Street, Lansing, IA 52151
Phone: 1-319-538-4500   1-800-397-0145

What Is My Postcard Worth?

By Jack Leach

In the not too distant past, this would have been a relatively easy question to answer. Your postcard would have had little monetary value. While postcards have been in existence for over a century, it is only in the last few decades that they have begun to acquire a monetary "value" other than for their philatelic interest. There were of course exceptions. Even at the 25th anniversary celebration of the postcard, held in 1894, there were collectors offering to pay premiums for certain cards. For the first 70 or 80 years of postcard history, the market in antique or secondary collector cards was very limited. Most people built their collections by purchasing new cards from postcard racks or shops. Others traded and bartered with fellow collectors. Actual sales of old postcards were usually limited to philatelic dealers and specialty shops such as book or manuscript dealers.

The start of the postcard market as we know it today began in the late 1940s following World War II. Postcard collecting activity became quite brisk during this period and peaked in the mid-1950s. During this time, several outstanding postcard clubs were formed. Postcard shows were started in many parts of the country, and collector interest grew. Also during this period, several books and manuals on postcard collecting were produced. Checklists and other research was initiated in many areas of the hobby and the future looked bright. While the postcard hobby continued to attract collectors after the mid-1950s, the momentum it had enjoyed was slowed. There were several reasons for the deceleration of growth in the hobby at this time. The expansion of television, which had its great growth during the 1950s was a challenge to every leisure time hobby. There was also competition from other hobbies. Numismatics and stamp collecting were just starting their large expansion and offered a more lucrative field for a hobby-oriented dealer. The most telling blow to the postcard hobby's expansion was probably its failure to establish a hobby publication of national scope. During the 1950s, there were many magazines and newspapers started concerning stamp and coin collecting. This gave public recognition and participation in these hobbies. No such national publications existed for postcards. The few publications that did exist performed a great service in preserving the hobby, but they were limited to a few collectors and did little to expose the hobby to the general public.

> While postcards have been in existence for over a century, it is only in the last few decades that they have begun to acquire a monetary "value" other than for their philatelic interest.

"What is my postcard worth?" In 1952, cards were showing some impressive gains over the almost nonexistent values of the 1930s. View cards sold 2/5 cents, with some of the better views trading for as much as 10 cents. Better greeting cards often commanded prices as high as 2/15 cents, and the rare examples going as high as 50 cents or $1. One collector, responding to an offer by a dealer to sell her cards, stated that her collection had grown to the point that she was only purchasing cards from one certain publisher. These cards were to be in excellent unused condition, and she would pay 5 cents each for them or give 30 cents for five at one time. While some cards commanded relatively high prices in the early 1950s, these were mainly limited to a $5 to $10 price range.

But while prices by today's standards were low, unless you happened to live in a large city, your opportunity to purchase collectible cards was almost nonexistent. Only a few antique dealers and stamp dealers bothered to stock postcards, and then it was usually a shoe box of cards thrown together with no attempt at categorizing the cards by subject.

"What is my postcard worth today?" This is not as easy a question to answer as it was previously. The past 20 years, and especially the last decade, have brought astonishing changes to the postcard hobby. When choreographing events that have led to a certain point in the growth of any hobby, there are those that are self-evident. Other events are easily overlooked that provided key pivots in the hobby's development. The postcard hobby today is a good example of such developments. There were changes that represented major turning points for the hobby. The first national magazines and hobby papers were started in the early 1980s; the formation of dealer organizations such as the International Federation of Postcard Dealers was such an event. Collector-oriented groups such as the International Postcard Association also represented real milestones in the growth of the hobby. Equally important are hundreds of minor events that have tended to shape the hobby—the decision to write that book, to work up that checklist, to start a postcard club, or to organize a show. The part-time postcard dealer who decides to devote full time to the hobby. The decision to drive that extra hundred miles to support a postcard show. The courage to start a postcard auction, when at best it would be a break-even venture in the beginning. All these "little events" combined with the major ones have brought us to where the hobby is today. Hundreds of postcard shows are taking place each year across the nation. There are now great numbers of professional postcard dealers. There are national publications that either pertain wholly or in part to postcard collecting, and there's the formation of a national postcard convention, having witnessed its second year in 1991. Scores of postcard clubs exist, with many new ones being formed each year. The postcard hobby has come a long way in the past few years, and its future seems bright. There is still a lot of work to be completed before the hobby reaches a greater degree of maturity, but the groundwork to date has been excellent.

What is yet to be done? For one thing, a simple answer to the title of this article, "What is my postcard worth today?" There has to be a comprehensive price guide updated on at least an annual basis. While some may argue that such an undertaking is impossible, several such foreign price guides already in existence illustrate that it is both practical and essential. The French price guide *Cartes Postales* and the English *IPM Catalogue of Picture Postcards* are two examples of practical guides. Another needed item is a practical guide to postcard grading. There must be a universal understanding of terms of condition be-

fore any hobby can reach maturity. More public awareness of the desirability and value of postcards is needed. A newsstand publication, be it one such as *Postcard Collector* or a new publication, would greatly increase the public's awareness and interest in postcards. Also needed are more books on postcards, more and improved dealer organizations, and bet-

═══════════════════════════════
The prices on these cards are indicative of both the overall quality of the images on different cards as well as the relative scarcity of certain cities and towns.
═══════════════════════════════

ter cooperation between show promoters on scheduling. These are a few of the things that would help achieve a more mature phase of a very worthwhile hobby.

So, what is my postcard worth? If your card is a view card, and it probably is, as over 50 percent of picture postcards are views, we will examine three time eras. If you card was printed between

1905-1935, it would have the following retail price range. Large city street scenes with animation (people, transportation, etc.) $2-$5 each. Large city street scenes without animation $1-$3 each. Large city buildings (schools, depots, courthouses, etc.) $1-$4 each. Large city parks and bridges 50 cents-$2 each. Small town street scenes with animation $3-$10 each, without animation $2-$6 each. Small town buildings $2-$6 each, small town parks and bridges $1-$3 each. These prices are for cards in collectible condition. Rural and scenic views with animation $1-$3 each, without animation 50 cents-$2 each. The prices on these cards are indicative of both the overall quality of the images on different cards as well as the relative scarcity of certain cities and towns. In most cases a card's price is midway of the price range. For example, small town parks and bridges have a range of $1-$3, and most cards would be about $2 each. Real photograph cards from this time frame follow the same guidelines but can average 50-100 percent higher, especially those examples with street scenes and store buildings. Also note that special topical matter included in view cards can greatly add to their value. Such topics include

famous people, special transportation, scarce signs, etc.

The second era of view cards we will examine are the linen type cards. These cards were printed primarily between 1930 and 1955, with most of their production occurring during and immediately after the war years. Scorned by many collectors until recently, the linen era postcards are quickly coming into their own. The same guidelines apply to linen view cards as to the older postcards, except they tend to be lower in price. Large city street scenes with animation $1-$3 each, without animation 50 cents-$2 each. Large city buildings 50 cents-$2 each, parks and bridges 50 cents-$1 each. Rural views and scenes with animation 50 cents-$2 each, without animation 25 cents-$1 each. The quality of the image on a linen card does affect the value. As a rule, the poorer quality large city, rural, and scenic views have very little demand and subsequently very little value. In general, the small town linen views are much more scarce so poor image quality is more easily forgiven and tend to command prices in line with the better quality linens. Real photo postcards from this time period tend to bring prices 50-100 percent higher than their counterparts in the linen type cards.

There is a special type of view card that makes its appearance in the linen era cards. These are the Roadside Americana cards illustrating motels, diners, service stations, etc. These cards came into their own during the Linen Era. Linen motel cards generally retail between $1-$3 depending on both the location and the quality of the image. Multiviews generally command higher prices. Restaurants are in the same price range, but diner cards tend to trade much higher. Most linen era diners are in the $5-$8 range, but it is not uncommon to find the rarer ones of the classic diners 100-200 percent higher. Service stations showing gas pumps and equipment are generally found in the $3-$6 range, but can go much higher for better quality and scarce examples. Even adding gas pumps to a motel or restaurant card can increase its value 25-50 percent.

The last time frame we will examine in view cards is the chrome era. These cards were have generally been produced from the early 1950s to the present. Most chrome era cards have retail values of 25-50 cents. However it is not uncommon to see early street scenes in the chrome era, those between 1950 and the mid-1960s bringing prices of $1-$2, especially if they show a lot of animation such as cars and people. Additionally the Roadside America theme continues into this era. The

prices on the chrome motels tend to be from 50 percent less to equal to the same type card from the linen era. The same holds true for the postcards illustrating diners and service stations.

The next type we will look at for evaluation purposes is the general greeting card. We will include in this group most holiday cards, humor cards, and museum type art reproduction cards. Since over 30 percent of all postcards by volume fall into the group, it will be the next logical place to find your postcard. We will examine two main time frames, the period between 1905 and 1915 and the period from 1916 to 1940.

> ## Most postcards have value. In many cases, the value may be more of a nostalgic nature than an actual monetary one.

In the first period, common holiday cards, which include Christmas, New Years, Easter, Birthday, and Thanksgiving, usually retail for 50 cents-$2. These cards with special topics illustrated, such as children, dolls, toys, etc., can run 50-100 percent higher, as can these cards by certain artists and publishers. Santa postcards are in a group by themselves and command $3-$10 as a rule. Santa cards by certain artists and publishers can bring $12-$45 and higher. Novelty Santa cards such as hold-to-lights can run several hundred dollars per card. The not so common holiday cards include Valentines Day, Fourth of July, Memorial Day, Decoration Day, Lincoln's Birthday, Washington's Birthday, St. Patrick's Day, April Fools Day, and other minor holidays. Most of the cards are priced retail $2-$10, but again certain artists and publishers bring higher prices. The rare holiday cards are Ground Hog Day cards (original, not after 1930), and Labor Day cards, which number six. Four Labor Day cards were made by Lounsbury Publishers and two by Nash. All of these cards are highly collectible and retail from $100-$450 each. Humor cards run from 50 cents-$3 each, but there are notable exceptions. Special topicals such as women's suffrage, prohibition, and blacks are all examples of topics that greatly add to the value of humor cards. Museum type art cards retail from 50 cents-$3 each, with the better publishers such as Stengel found in the upper end of the price range. Special topicals such as art nudes can run 50-100 percent higher. With the exception of Judaic cards, most religious-related cards are in the 50 cent-$2 range. Exceptions

also include famous religious leaders and cards by certain artists.

The holiday and humor cards published in the second time frame, 1916-1940, follow the same guidelines as the first period except the prices tend to be 25-50 percent lower in most cases. In general, the quality of printing after World War I did not equal that of pre-war years. Also the sending of postcards on holidays was greatly curtailed, and after 1930 almost ceased.

The linen era saw humor cards attain a new height of interest. The bright art deco style of the linen cards produced some very outstanding humor cards. Linen humor cards have gained a growing collector base in recent years. Cards that were selling for 25 cents each just two or three years ago bring several times that today. Most linen humor cards are priced 50 cents-$2, with better topicals such as pinups and military humor bringing $2-$5 each or higher.

Chrome humor and greeting cards, 1950s to present, are generally priced 25-50 cents for desirable cards. Art related chrome cards and most topicals are in the same price range.

So far, we have covered cards that make up most of the United States-produced postcards (80+ percent). For the purpose of evaluating your card, we are not taking into account foreign-related cards. If your card came to you by inheritance, was given to you, or one you picked up years ago or bought in a yard sale, hopefully we have managed to evaluate your card. If not, the odds of your card being a "better" card increases.

While there are hundreds of categories still uncovered, two very important ones should be mentioned. Advertising cards and non-museum type art cards, better known as artist signed cards. Advertising postcards are the most common of the two and have the most diverse range and time span.

Postcards were first produced in the United States in 1873 (excepting the Lipman postal cards), and they were U.S. government cards. The first advertising overprints were produced soon after that date using government issue cards. Private postcards appeared as early as 1874, and they were also of an advertising nature. Advertising postcards have played an active role in shaping United States social history as they have been used to promote almost every cause. From presidential candidates to local politicians, postcards have been utilized to promote their ad campaigns. There is no simple rule in determining the value of your postcard if it happens to be an advertising card. The price range on advertising cards runs from 50 cents to over $1,000 each. Most early ad cards (1905-1940) fall into the $3-$8 price range. Some of the most prolific of the early, common, advertising are the Kellogg Company Niagara Falls cereal cards and the H.J. Heinz Company Atlantic City Ocean Pier Cards. Some of the better known rarities include the two early Coca Cola cards, the Mucha "Warner Corset" cards, and the Bloomingdales Department Store ad cards by the artist Outcault. These top end advertising cards range from $100-$800 each and higher.

The price range of artist signed postcards also varies greatly. The most commonly collected American artists are Philip Boileau and Harrison Fisher. Their cards run from $12-$25, but certain scarce series and types can command much higher prices. The famous American series by the Fidler sisters, Pearl and Alice, are priced $8-$15. The Fidler postcards are a favorite of collectors because of their beautiful watercolors. The price range of $2-$10 finds postcards produced by artists such as Bernhardt Wall, Charles Twelvetrees, and Walter Wellman, to name a few. Many artists' postcards will bring a wide range of values. One example is Ellen Clapsaddle. The Clapsaddle postcards range from common holiday types, $1-$3 each, to better holiday cards that can run as high as $6-$12, as well as special topical cards such as Santas that can run even higher.

While space precludes mentioning all card categories, we need to draw some conclusions from those we have listed. Most postcards have value. In many cases, the value may be more of a nostalgic nature than an actual monetary one. If you have doubts about the value of your card, seek an appraisal. See if you have a local postcard club. Almost any member will be happy to assist you. Visit a postcard show in your area. There you will find both dealers and collectors to assist you. If there are indications that your postcard may be valuable, solicit several opinions. Often a card may be outside a certain person's field of expertise. Don't be disappointed if your card isn't a rarity. Only a very small percentage of postcards fall into the rare classification. Even if your postcard is not an object of great monetary value, it may become a cherished family heirloom in the coming years.

We will close with some additional thoughts about grade and condition to realize a top price. It is often hard for the non-collector to grasp the necessity for quality condition of collectibles. When collecting material objects, there is a desire to obtain the finest condition possible. Postcard collectors are no different. Whether assembling a minor collection of just a few postcards or a major collection involving up to hundreds of thousands of cards, the collector has devoted time, effort, and probably money to assemble the cards. It is only natural that the collector wants this effort to reflect a collection they can take pride in. For this reason many collectors will try to "upgrade" their collections, replacing lower grade or damaged cards with better condition ones when the opportunity presents itself. Most dealers realize the reluctance of collectors to purchase low grade or damaged cards and are hesitant to place such cards in their inventory. So if your postcard has problems, do not expect to receive a high evaluation even though you might otherwise have a scarce and valuable card.

About the Author

The postcard values expressed in this article are retail prices. See "How to Sell Your Postcards" in this edition of the Postcard Collector Annual *for a scale of prices that a seller can expect to be paid by dealers, relative to retail values. Questions pertaining to the prices expressed in this article can be directed to the author, Jack Leach, c/o National Postcard Exchange, 225 Third Street/ P.O. Box 886, Macon, Georgia 31202-0886.*

POSTCARD COLLECTOR

1990

Customer Service Award Recipients

Abraham's Corner
American Historic Society
Anthony's
Bag Man, The
Bowers, Dave
Braynard, Frank O.
Budd, Ellen H.
Card Collectors Co., The
Cherryland PC Auction
Coupe, George
Cox, Roy
Dobres, S.
Fred & Gail's Modern PC
Grab Bag Antiques
Greater Chicago PC Show
Hanson, Bill & Marilyn
I.F.P.D.
La Posta Publications
Landmark Postcards
Majorstamps
Manochio & Sons
Martin, Ltd., Mary

McClintock Postcard Sales
Memory Lane Postcards
Metropolitan PC Club
Millns Postcards
Modern Postcard Sales
National PC Exchange
Novick, Richard
Numismatic Card Co.
Postcards International
R & M Postcards
R & N Postcard Co.
Raskin Shows, Marty
San Francisco Bay Shows
Schryver, Jane
Service Printing Co.
Shiloh Postcards
Show Promotion, Inc.
Springston, EK
SW Michigan PC Club
Tippett, Inc.
Windy City PC Club

The **Customer Service Award** is an acknowledged symbol of honesty and integrity in postcard dealing and is based on the following criteria:
- No complaints outstanding at the end of 1990 and no more than two complaints registered during the year;
- All test order materials received as described;
- Display ads appeared in at least four issues during 1990;
- Display advertising space accumulated to at least 40 column inches during 1990* (* Some restrictions apply);
- All advertising paid in full;
- And other criteria, as appropriate.

Postcards Move to Retail Book Shelves

By Jennifer Henderson

Postcards have moved off the rack and onto retail book shelves as publishers realize the sales potential from postcard assortments, compiled into neat booklike packages. With an abundance of topics, card sizes, paper stocks, bindings, and prices, these postcard books are a welcome addition to book store inventories. During last December's holiday shopping season, Santa's sack overflowed with postcard books whose themes varied from humor, pets, and recipes to works of art, rock 'n roll trivia, and reproductions of Christmas postcards from decades long past.

As nostalgic picture books, studies of distinct architectural styles, or flashes through someone's warped sense of humor, these book-form postcards are quite collectible; yet, they're also fun to give and are easily torn apart to send individually.

Prices for postcard books vary considerably, but most range between $4.95 to $8.95 for 24 to 32 cards. The major postcard book publishers: Pomegranate Artbooks in San Francisco, Peregrine Smith in Utah, Pantheon Books in New York, and Running Press in Philadelphia, prefer perfect binding in the manner of *Reader's Digest*. Preservation Press in Washington, D.C., puts out perfect bound "Past-Age" postcard books in cooperation with the Curt Teich Collection, although the cards are printed two across and smaller in size.

Other types of binding include metal spirals on *The World's Tackiest Postcards* ($5.95 from Klutz Press in Palo Alto, CA) and plastic spirals as used on *The Cookies Are Coming* ($4.95 from Waldman House Press in Minneapolis). Dover "ready-to-mail" postcard books are saddled-stitched (like *Newsweek*), generally measure 9 inches by 12 inches, feature 24 cards printed four per page, and run $3.50 to $3.95.

Flipping through postcard books, you can find examples of "19th and 20th century women and men who left a mark on their times and were also gay" (30 *Gay*

From Housewives in Hell, *a postmodern postcard book™ by Running Press, Philadelphia.*

Portraits cost $8.95 from Pomegranate); kids at the library (issued by the American Library Association, *Children & Public Libraries* contains 12 cards for $6.95); funky 1950s-1960s spoofs labeled *Lust For Shoes* and *Housewives in Hell* (30 "postmodern" cards per title for $7.95 from American Postcard Company, published by Running Press); and *Nostalgic Barbie* joining her doll friends at the beach, shopping, and traveling (30 cards for $7.95, also from American Postcard Company). Photographs of fighter planes, loons, teddy bears, blues musicians, North American mushrooms, Alaskan vistas, and glamorous Hollywood movie stars interested some publisher enough to turn them into postcard anthologies.

To please aging baby boomers, rock 'n roll memories fill several postcard books. Take a visual listen to *Top of the Charts: The 50s* for the "1950s musicians whose songs reached number 1 on the pop charts" (30

cards for $7.95). Pomegranate also issued a similar version for 1960s hits. *Rip It Up!* by Pantheon has 31 oversized "tear-and-send" postcards for $8.95, which feature mementos like record jackets, concert programs, fanzines, and posters, along with rock trivia on the flip side.

Art prospers in postcard books. Whether individual artists, collected paintings on a certain subject, or a particular type of art, each compilation puts a miniature art gallery of mailable masterpieces on your shelf. Within their pages, you can learn about Alphonse Mucha and his famously priced designs in Dover Book's *Original Mucha Postcards* (24 cards for $3.95); view graphically exciting labels in *Orange Crate Art* published by Running Press (30 cards for $7.95); study neon creations in *Liquid Fire* from Peregrine Smith (30 cards for $7.95); or tour Paris Metro stations through the Art Nouveau designs of Hector Guimard (20 cards for

$7.95, also from Peregrine Smith). Stunningly beautiful artworks in watercolor and gouache, acrylic and oil paints, colored pencils and collage are incorporated in *30 Contemporary Women Artists* (30 cards for $8.95 from Pomegranate). Unwilling to tear this treasured book apart, I had to buy an extra copy for sharing cards through the mail.

Chronicle Books in San Francisco dreamed up a novel way to keep your cards and send them too. They published a little hardcover edition called *Postcats* that blends delicate paintings of tabbies, calicos, and Siamese by Lesley Anne Ivory with feline poetry and verse. These same beautiful cats, each resting on handmade quilts, tapestry, lace, or mosaic, were then printed as postcards. The 15 cards and 32-page book are packaged in an attractive folder. At $10.95, this makes a lovely gift for cat-loving friends.

Garfield postcards have been available for years; now his familiar face fills a book of birthday postcards. *Greeting from the Sewer* comes from the Teenage Mutant Ninja Turtles. Those bellicose, pizza-gnawing hardshells instruct the buyer to "do the write thing—scrawl on 'em, stamp 'em, send 'em!" (24 radical cards from Random House go for $4.95.) Matt Groening's cartoons first gained attention with Binky, Bongo, Akbar, and Jeff in the *Life in Hell* series. In 1989, Pantheon published *Greetings from Hell* to showcase these bizarre characters. Groening's fame skyrocketed with Bart Simpson and his family, so *Greetings from the Simpsons* jumped onto book shelves last year in time for Christmas (32 oversized cards for $8.95 from HarperCollins in New York).

A new twist on postcard books is definitely meant for sending rather than collecting. *EarthCards* are "postcards you can sign and send to save the earth." Published by the Write for Action Group, each postcard is preaddressed with a targeted message to the specific addressee whose products, or by-products, have some adverse impact on the environment. Without any hassle, you can send a card to the CEO of Scott Paper, DuPont stockholders, or 30 other consumer companies, automobile factories, banks, airlines, and politicians.

With such a variety of topics, where retailers stock postcard books is arbitrary. Be sure to check several sections of the shop such as among the nature books, children's books—where a lone Sierra Club title, *Young Animals*, had been stashed—cartoon collections, and cookbooks. Who knows how long this current trend will last, so shop soon!

P.S. If you get to Chicago, the best selection I've found in upstairs at Rizzoli Bookstore in Water Tower Place.

About the Author

Jennifer Henderson, feature writer and columnist for Postcard Collector, *specializes in recipe postcards and runs a postcard mail-order service, "Cookin' With Postcards."*

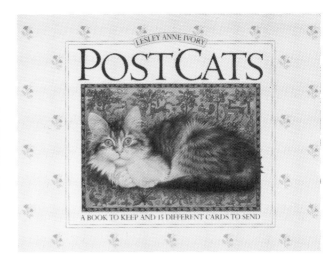

Published by Chronicle Books, San Francisco.

Published by Pomegranate Artbooks, San Francisco.

The Simpsons™ © 1990 by Matt Groening Productions, Inc. Published by HarperCollins.

NATIONAL **P**OSTCARD **C**OLLECTOR **C**ONVENTION

3rd Annual

MAY 22-23, 1992

MECCA Convention Center

Downtown Milwaukee, 500 W. Kilbourn Avenue

Milwaukee, WI

MORE OF THE BEST

(Watch Postcard Collector Magazine for Details.)

For Show Information Contact:

MAGGIE JONES

National Postcard Collector Convention

P.O. Box 337
Iola, WI 54945
715-445-5000

How to Sell Your Postcards

By Jonah Shapiro

"Wow! I found all these boxes of old (and valuable) postcards in the attic of the house I just purchased."

*****

"I've had fun with my cards for 25 years. I guess it's time to sell them."

*****

"I bought 1,400 cards from auction offerings, carefully one by one, and never paid over 25 percent of the estimated value. Now I'm going to cash them in and go on that trip to the islands."

*****

"My mom had so much fun collecting cards. Now that they've been left to me, I just want to sell them for a fair price."

*****

In these and similar situations, the question is: how *does* one sell such collections or accumulations? Not only is the "best" price wanted, but considerations should include the desire for a minimum of headaches and, often, quick settlement.

To find the right answer, it is useful to know that cards are generally marketed by dealers to collectors in several different ways. This knowledge can be helpful in choosing the most effective marketer of one's own cards.

Most cards are sold to collectors by the following methods:
• Auctions, mail bid or public
• Approvals
• Fixed price lists:
  1. House organs 2. Display ads
• Bourse table sales

If one does not want to become a dealer and try to sell the cards piecemeal (fun, hard work, and probably not the best way to get the most, especially if one figures one's time is worth over 25 cents per hour!), one has to decide to trust a professional: a postcard dealer, auctioneer, or some other kind of postcard retailer. (Most definitely do not use a non-postcard merchant to market postcards for you.) Dealers who use the maximum number of the above-outlined methods of selling are good bets for handling a diverse holding. Read up a bit on cards, but place more emphasis on finding out about the dealer than about the cards. Fortunately, integrity is rarely a problem in this hobby, so look for experience and reputation.

Very few dealers can pay outright for a very large collection or accumulation

1: Foreign "local color." 2: Printed view card. 3: General greeting. Here are three cards typical of what can be found in great numbers in large accumulations. They are commercially of insignificant value, even though "old" and "attractive."

(often worth upwards of $30,000.) But you can maximize your return by carefully consigning the cards in sizable chunks, allowing the dealer to pay as he/she sells. As long as there is a deposit-clinched guarantee of a minimum amount to be finally realized, with perhaps a sliding scale, upwards, of additional amounts to be paid to you once the minimum has been reached and more cards still left to be sold, you will be adequately protected. This is to preclude the selling off of the "best" stuff first, and then being told later, of the balance, "well, I can't really sell these in 'this' market, etc.," so that one gets back the dross, along with a whole new set of selling problems.

The publication you are reading is replete with ads from dealers, large and small. Visit one nearest you, or make a phone call and request a visit. Do not expect a free appraisal or random bid ("free" information will be worth *less* than you pay for it). Discuss your holding, and ask what the dealer suggests. Size up the dealer during this visit. Go with your common sense, taking into consideration the above-outlined strategies. Be sincere with your prospective "partner," and you will find that you will be happy with yourself and the results.

If you are not in a hurry, subscribe to *Postcard Collector*, read the ads in a few issues to get an idea which dealer you want to approach. Then visit and/or call. Or go to a postcard show in your section of the country, and interview several dealers, choosing those whose ads and prior recommendations have appealed to you. Get a feel for the quality of the dealer while at the show, and then negotiate seriously with the one or two that show the attributes of professionalism required to get the job done properly for you.

Appraisals

It can be useful to have your cards appraised by a competent dealer, preferably one who will back up the appraisal with an offer to buy. Very often inexpert appraisals are obtained, which prove to be misleading to the owner because no one is willing to actually pay the appraised value! However, appraisals take time, and the appraiser has the right to be paid for the service. Frequently the appraisal fee is waived if the collection is subsequently sold to the appraiser. There is at least one widely advertised free appraisal service which is bonafide; it is offered by a full-time professional dealer.

Because postcard collections and accumulations are frequently very bulky, it is physically difficult to present them to potential buyers or appraisers. Small lots can safely be mailed (get posting receipts), but the big ones require the interested party traveling (expensive) to see your

A card of artistic strength and featuring a topic (sports) in considerable demand.

cards. Again, be prepared to pay these costs. At best, they will be deducted from the final figure arrived at. It can be useful to mail a segment of the lot for the potential buyer to inspect, to see if further steps toward getting together are worthwhile for both sides of the transaction. The practice of mailing small lots for offers to test the buyer may result in a distorted picture, since the entire lot's worth can vary significantly from what a small segment suggests.

Do not waste your time compiling long descriptive lists if you are basically unfamiliar with cards: such lists usually go into the wastebasket! It would be more practical to photocopy a cross section of the cards (not hundreds of them!) and suggest that they are representative of what you have. Do not ask for quotes (bids) on these cards, but rather use the photocopies as an introduction to a hopefully fruitful dialogue.

Selling to the Collector

Now let's talk about another outlet for your cards, as a lot: the collector. Seemingly, a collector should pay more for a collection than a dealer. This is frequently true FOR THOSE CARDS WANTED BY A COLLECTOR FOR HIS COLLECTION. But probably only a small percentage of your cards would fit into any one collector's specialty. So, the collector would have the same need to find a method of disposing of the bulk of the lot bought from you after the few cards he really wants are abstracted, and he would most likely figure as much when making you his offer.

There are, however, some collectors who would want to "work with" your cards, just for the fun of it. In this happy case, you would have found an outlet that

could, with patience, net you a decent price for your cards. However, you are cautioned to get a professional estimate first, and get some sort of guaranty from your buyer that you will net at least this amount as a minimum within a specific time frame. As in the case of getting interest on funds, it may not be wise to give up security (a firm deal) for a point or two extra.

Evaluating Your Cards

Although this article does not propose to tell you how to evaluate your cards (this is done elsewhere in this annual), sellers usually want to have at least a rough idea of what cards are worth in general before accepting an offer or method of selling.

Because most cards are very inexpensive compared to other collectibles, a total of catalog values does not give the owner a meaningful indication of what he can really get for the cards: the cost of handling by a dealer can be a very high percentage of the ultimate "retail" value. For example, it is not infrequent for card hoards to contain tens of thousands of cards. If looked up in a catalog, or on an auction prices realized list, of the first 100 cards studied, many may be "worth" $2-$3 each. "Well," you say, "let's be realistic; let's cut the average in half. Say, $1.25 each. Now 50,000 x $1.25, hmmm, wow (!)...that's over $60,000 in these shoe boxes. I'll let the dealer make a *good* profit. So I should get at least $25,000 to $30,000 quickly." But, be advised, similar lots actually turn over for under 20 cents a card quite frequently, dealer to dealer!

On the other hand, such unpicked old-time lots often times do have real treasures tucked among the quantity stuff. Yet, if these are separated out, the average price per card for the vast bulky remainder may now only obtain under 10 cents per card! This may result in a much lower total realization than if the better cards were left in and all sold as a lot.

In one of the introductory paragraphs in what is the foremost postcard catalog in the world (Neudin...French), the author advises the reader to pay attention to the following scale of prices to expect to be paid by dealers for cards, relative to retail prices. He suggests that following this scale will help avoid disappointment and disillusionment:

•Cards retailing at less than $4 each, divide the price by 10. (On very ordinary lots, do not expect more than 15 cents per card, on semi-moderns, 5 cents per card, and 2 cents for moderns.)
•Cards retailing $4 to $12, divide by 5.
•Cards retailing $12 to $30, divide by 3.
•Cards retailing $30 to $100, divide by 2.
•Cards retailing over $100, about 1/3 off retail.

It is not suggested that you try to ascertain the retail value of all your cards before selling (this can be a frustrating and debilitating exercise), but it is good to be aware that a merchant will most likely figure the buying price based quite closely on the above guidelines.

We have spoken here at length about old-time collections or hoards. Strange as

Do not be unduly impressed by the age of the collection when seeking to sell inherited cards.

it may seem at first, a collection built within the past decade will frequently be smaller but much more valuable than the "old" collection. In years past, when cards traded for one to 15 cents per card, collectors sought quantity and rarely developed sophisticated taste. The vast majority of cards produced were of rather pedestrian nature, and the old-time lots are made up mostly of cards which even today bring not much more than when first produced and/or collected. The contemporary active collectors, paying more per card, have frequently been selective and specialist oriented, and have more likely built collections of cards more acceptable and in demand in the current market channels. So do not be unduly impressed by the age of the collection when seeking to sell inherited cards.

Although it was indicated in this article other outlets for the disposal a collection (by selling to a collector, or by becoming a dealer yourself), we have concentrated on the most practical way of selling, to a dealer, and we have made suggestions as to how to select the proper one for you. It is somewhat like selling a home: using an established agency generally is a much more satisfactory way to achieve satisfying "market" value than "doing it yourself." Realize that the dealer must make a decent profit and allow him/her to operate freely. Get sound guaranties of total payment, and then...let it flow.

About the Author

Jonah Shapiro, founder of Postcards International, P.O. Box 2930, New Haven, CT 06515, specializes in the buying and selling of quality postcards. Professional consultations are available by appointment.

"Pretty" greeting cards, pre-1920. Again, these cards are found in great quantities in collections, but are of very little worth and demand.

Postcard Club Roster

The purpose of this club roster is to provide contacts for prospective members. The data published in this roster was verified during the first two months of 1991. We thank the club officers who checked and corrected the data and returned the forms. Only clubs responding to the questionnaire are listed. Members active in clubs not listed are welcome to submit data for an update to be published in the 1992 *Postcard Collector Annual*. Persons interested in participating in a local club are urged to contact the officers of a group near them. Although meeting sites and times have been included, it's important to call ahead to verify this information for last-minute changes. Clubs are usually non-profit groups. If requesting a response in writing, be sure to include an SASE.

ARIZONA
Arizona Post Card Club
Founded 1986
Terry Pavey, Pres.
7018 W. Josac, Glendale, AZ 85308
Dick Callender, Memb.
6330 E. Avalon Dr., Scottsdale, AZ 85251
PH: 602-945-8387
Dues: $5.00
State Democratic Headquarters
1525 N. Central Ave., Phoenix, AZ
Second Wednesday, 7:00pm
Quarterly Newsletter, Annual Roster
Tucson Post Card Exchange Club
Founded 1990
Joan Gentry, Pres.
Stan Spurgiesz, Memb.
3338 E. Waverly St., Tucson, AZ 85716
PH: 602-325-1258
Dues: $10.00, $2.00 Additional Family Members
First Sunday, 2:00pm

ARKANSAS
Arkansas Postcard Club
Ralph Allen, Pres.
P.O. Box 2413, Little Rock, AR 72203
PH: 501-834-1733
Sam Storthz III, Memb.
20 Shannon Dr., Little Rock, AR 72207
Dues: $5.00, $8.00 Family
Laman Library
North Little Rock, AR
Second Thursday, 7:00pm
Monthly Newsletter, Annual Roster

CALIFORNIA
Northern California Post Card Club
E. Jeane Campfield, Pres. & Memb.
1200 Douglas Lane, Redding, CA 96002
PH: 916-222-6232
Dues: None
Second Saturday
Call for Meeting Location & Time
San Diego Postcard Club
Sally Fall, Pres.
P.O. Box 591, La Jolla, CA 92038
Ken DeHahn, Memb.
645 Melrose Ave., Chula Vista, CA 91910
PH: 619-422-5925
Dues: $7.00, $8.00 Family
North Clairmont Recreation Center
4421 Bannock Ave., Room #2, San Diego, CA 92117
Third Tuesday, 6:00pm
San Francisco Bay Area Postcard Club
Founded 1985
Jim Kurshuk, Pres. & Memb.
1951 Eddy St., San Francisco, CA 94115
PH: 415-931-8936
Dues: $10.00, $12.00 Family, $15.00 Foreign
Fort Mason Center
Bay & Laguna Sts., San Francisco, CA
Fourth Saturday Except December, 12:00noon
Annual Roster, 11 Newsletters Per Year
Annual Show
San Jose Post Card Club
Walter Kransky, Pres.
P.O. Box 32628, San Jose, CA 95152-2628
Laura Silverman, Memb.
P.O. Box 32628, San Jose, CA 95152-2628
Dues: $6.00, $13.00 Foreign
Rose Garden Library
1580 Naglee Ave., San Jose, CA
Second Tuesday, September Through June, 6:30pm
Annual Roster, 5 Newsletters Per Year
Annual Show, Spring
Santa Cruz Post Card Club
Joseph Jaynes, Pres.
2-1226 E. Cliff Dr., Santa Cruz, CA 95062
PH: 408-476-3262
Shirley Lopes, Memb.
452 Los Altos Dr., Aptos, CA 95003
PH: 408-688-5897
Dues: $6.00
Seacliff Mobile Home Park
2700 Mar Vista Dr., Aptos, CA
First Monday, 7:00pm
Monthly Newsletter
Santa Monica Postcard Club
Lee Brown, Pres.
P.O. Box 92, Sunland, CA 91041
PH: 818-352-5663, 818-896-7919
Marshall Siskin, Memb.
1441 4th St., Santa Monica, CA 90401
Dues: $6.00, $1.00 Each Additional Family Member
Fairview Branch Library
2101 Ocean Park Blvd, Santa Monica, CA
First Thursday, 6:30pm
Monthly Meeting Notice
Call Dee Teitzell for directions, 213-450-2665
Torrance-South Bay Post Card Collectors
John Salerno, Pres. & Memb.
805 Via Los Miradores, Redondo Beach, CA 90277
Dues: $5.00, $6.00 Family
Mercury Savings
22939 Hawthorne Blvd., Torrance, CA
Last Sunday, 2:00pm
Monthly Newsletter, Annual Roster

COLORADO
Denver Post Card Club
Foxy, Pres.
P.O. Box 260170, Lakewood, CO 80226-0170
George Van Trump, Memb.
P.O. Box 260170, Lakewood, CO 80226-0170
PH: 303-985-3508
Dues: $6.00, $7.00 Family
Econo-Lodge
1800 W. Sheri Lane, Littleton, CO
Second Sunday, 1:30pm
Monthly Newsletter, Annual Roster

CONNECTICUT
Connecticut Post Card Club
Founded 1954
Tom Dickau, Pres.
33 Fenway Ave., Bristol, CT 06010
Bill & Candie Callan, Memb.
340 Moose Hill Rd., Monroe, CT 06468
PH: 203-261-5058
Dues: $6.00, $4.00 Each Additional Family Member
Knights of Columbus Hall
2630 Whitney Ave., Hamden, CT
Third Sunday, 10:00am
Quarterly Newsletter, Annual Roster
Annual Show

FLORIDA
Sunshine Postcard Club
Lyn Friedt, Pres.
2236 Highland St. S., St. Petersburg, FL 33705
PH: 813-823-4215
Dorothy Bruns, Memb.
210 6th Ave. N., St. Petersburg, FL 33701
PH: 813-823-4060
Dues: $8.00, $1.00 Additional Family Members, $11.00 Canadian, $15.00 Foreign
Clearwater Garden Club Hall
Ft. Harrison Ave. & Seminole St., Clearwater, FL
First Saturday—April, June, August, December, 10:00am
Bimonthly Newsletter, 2 Shows Per Year—February & October
Club Address: P.O. Box 1232, St. Petersburg, FL 33731

Tropical Post Card Club
Founded 1979
Tom Moore, Pres.
P.O. Box 431131, South Miami, FL
    33243-1131
Marvin Shapiro, Memb.
7521 S.W. 58th Ave., South Miami, FL
    33143
PH: 305-667-3936, 305-665-1333
Dues: $8.00, $2.00 Each Additional
    Family Member, $10.00 Canada,
    $16.00 Foreign
Royal Palm Clubhouse
545 N.E. 22nd Ave., Boynton Beach, FL
First Sunday, 12:00 Noon
Quarterly Newsletter, Annual Roster
2 Shows Per Year

GEORGIA

Georgia Postcard Club
Albert K. Schoenbucher, Pres.
765 Fairfield Dr., Marietta, GA 30068-
    4105
PH: 404-973-6915
Harry Rusche, Memb.
1436 Cornell Rd. N.E., Atlanta, GA
    30306
PH: 404-378-5035
Dues: $7.00
Decatur Recreation Center
231 Sycamore St., Decatur, GA
Third Saturday, 11:00am
Quarterly Bulletin "Georgia Peach,"
    Annual Roster
Dealer/Program Alternate at Meetings
2 Shows Per Year, Spring & Fall

ILLINOIS

Black Hawk Post Card Club
Founded 1980
Vickie Wetzel, Pres.
1325 45 St., Rock Island, IL 61201
PH: 309-786-1335
Arretta Wetzel
1325 45 St., Rock Island, IL 61201
PH: 309-786-1335
Dues: $6.00, $1.00 Additional Family
    Members
Hauberg Civic Center
13th Ave. & 24th St., Rock Island, IL
Union Federal S & L (May-July)
Rt. 67 & Andalusia Rd., Milan, IL
Third Thursday Except August & De-
    cember, 6:30pm
Bimonthly Newsletter, Annual Roster
Annual Show, Third Sunday in March
Corn Belt Philatelic Society, Inc.
Jack Jenkins, Pres.
Box 625, Bloomington, IL 61702-0625
PH: 309-663-2761
Janice Jenkins, Memb.
Box 625, Bloomington, IL 61702-0625
PH: 309-663-2761
Dues: $6.00, $1.00 Each Additional
    Family Member
Champion Federal Savings & Loan
115 E. Washington St., Bloomington, IL
Last Wednesday Except July Picnic &

December, 7:00pm
Monthly Newsletter, Annual Show
Homewood Flossmoor Post Card Club
Richard Barnes, Pres.
Les Lawitz, Memb.
18820 Highland Ave., Homewood, IL
    60430
PH: 312-957-0874
Dues: $5.00, $7.50 Family
Dolphin Lake Clubhouse
183rd St. & Governors Highway,
    Homewood, IL
Second Tuesday, 7:30pm
10 Newsletters Per Year, Annual Show
Meeting Place Varies Occasionally
Rock Valley Postcard Club
Founded 1983
Robert Swanson, Pres.
924 17th St., Rockford, IL 61104
PH: 815-398-5384
Molly Crocker, Memb.
P.O. Box 2722, Rockford, IL 61132-2722
PH: 815-282-5166
Dues: $4.00
Belvidere Public Library
320 North State St., Belvidere, IL 61008
Third Wednesday, 7:00pm
Quarterly Newsletter
2 Shows Per Year, April & November
Windy City Post Card Club
John Belka, Pres.
P.O. Box 818, La Grange, IL 60525
Marianne Matthews, Memb.
P.O. Box 818, La Grange, IL 60525
Dues: $7.50, $3.50 Additional Family
    Members, $10.00 Foreign
Sokol Hall
3909 S. Prairie Ave., Brookfield, IL
First Wednesday, 7:00pm
Bimonthly Newsletter, Bienniel Roster
Annual Show

INDIANA

Maple City Postcard Club
Founded 1969
Albert Hornberger, Pres.
218 River Vista Dr., Goshen, IN 46526
PH: 219-533-1340
Clara Reed, Memb.
2000 W. Wilden, Lot #136, Goshen, IN
    46526
First National Bank, Eastside Branch
2000 Middlebury St., Elkhart, IN
First Thursday, 7:30pm
Annual Show, March
Contact Thomas Zollinger, 219-522-
    3954, or Modern Postcards Sales,
    219-264-0013 for information.
Indianapolis Post Card Club
Founded 1974
Joseph Seiter, Pres.
2117 Winchester Dr., Indianapolis, IN
    46224
PH: 317-888-8475
Grace Perkoski, Memb.
3502 Moller Rd., Indianapolis, IN
    46224
PH: 317-297-5611

Dues: $5.00, $6.00 Family
7th & 8th United Christian Church
2916 W. 30th At Medford, Indianapo-
    lis, IN
Second Thursday, 7:30pm
Bimonthly Bulletin, Annual Roster
Annual Show
Twin Bridges Postcard Club
Sarah Cooper, Pres.
Elsie Phillips, Memb.
536 S. Kerth Ave., Evansville, IN 47714
PH: 812-423-1811
Dues: $5.00
McCurdy Residential Center, Embers
    Room
101 SE 1st St., Evansville, IN
Second Monday, 6:00pm
Annual Roster, 2-3 Newsletters Per
    Year
Annual Show, April

IOWA

Cedar Rapids Postcard Club
Wally Searcy, Pres.
3240 Whittier Rd., Springville, IA 52336
PH: 319-854-7359
Vivian Rinaberger, Memb.
4548 Fairlane Dr. NE, Cedar Rapids, IA
    52402
PH: 319-393-6743
Dues: $4.00, $7.00 Family
Members' Homes
Call for dates and times
Bimonthly Newsletter, Annual Roster
2 Shows Per Year, May & October
Cheerio Post Card Club
Gladys Swaim, Memb.
Box 6, Webb, IA 51366
PH: 712-838-4365
Dues: $2.00
Public Library
Spencer, IA
Second Monday, 1:00pm
Hawkeye Postcard Club
Founded 1978
Wesley Phillippi, Pres.
3111 40th St., Des Moines, IA 50310
PH: 515-279-7972
Agnes Aller, Memb.
2001 53rd St., Des Moines, IA 50310
PH: 515-279-5418
Dues: $5.00
Calvin West Apartments Activity Room
4210 Hickman Rd., Des Moines, IA
    50310
Third Thursday, 7:00pm
Quarterly Newsletter, Annual Roster
Annual Show, 4th Saturday in
    September
Iowa's Wildrose Postcard Club
David A. Wilson, Pres.
836 Lynkaylee Dr., Waterloo, IA 50701
PH: 319-232-2506
Laura Fox, Memb.
721 2nd Ave., Evansdale, IA 50707
Hawkeye Institute of Technology
211 Grundy Hall, Waterloo, IA 50701
Third Monday, 7:00pm

Post Card Pals
Founded 1972
Betty Weiland, Pres. & Memb.
2324 Maplewood Dr., Dubuque, IA
    52001
PH: 319-583-8342
Emmaus Bible College
2570 Asbury, Dubuque, IA
Second Thursday, 7:00pm

KANSAS
Wichita Postcard Club
Founded 1977
Beverly Henline, Pres.
107 E. 16th, Wichita, KS 67214
PH: 316-267-2534
Dorothy L. Johnson, Memb.
P.O. Box 780282, Wichita, KS 67278-
    0282
Dues: $8.00, $1.00 Each Additional
    Family Member
Wichita Public Library
South Main, Wichita, KS
Alternating Between First Tuesday
    Evening & First Saturday Afternoon
    Each Month
Monthly Newsletter, Annual Roster
Annual Show, October

MAINE
Pine Tree Post Card Club
Founded 1978
Joseph LePage, Pres.

P.O. Box 6815, Portland, ME 04101
Earl Tibbetts, Memb.
P.O. Box 6815, Portland, ME 04101
PH: 207-775-2716
Dues: $5.00
Portland Public Safety Bldg.
109 Middle St., Portland, ME
Second Monday, 7:00pm
Quarterly Newsletter
3 Shows Per Year, May, July, October

MARYLAND
Capitol Beltway Postcard Club
Founded 1976
Tony Chaves, Pres.
P.O. Box 366, Falls Church, VA 22040
PH: 703-560-0237
Harold Silver, Memb.
39 Landsend Dr., Gaithersburg, MD
    20878
Dues: $5.00, $7.00 Couple, $15.00
    Dealer
Greenbelt Middle School
8950 Edmonston Rd., Greenbelt, MD
Second Thursday Except July &
    August, 7:00pm
Monthly Newsletter, Annual Roster
Monumental Postcard Club
Dee Delcher, Pres.
Bob Baker, Memb.
P.O. Box 9775, Baltimore, MD 21284
Dues: $8.00 Single, $10.00 Family,

$20.00 Foreign
Star Community Hall
7405 Windsor Mill Rd., Baltimore, MD
    21207
4th Sunday, 1:00pm
Monthly Newssheet, Biennial Roster
Annual Show

MASSACHUSETTS
Bay State Postcard Collectors Club
Founded 1949
John Vierra, Pres.
P.O. Box 6783, Portland, ME 04101
PH: 207-657-4399
Anne Crane, Memb.
P.O. Box 334, Lexington, MA 02173
PH: 617-646-3576
Dues: $7.00
Elks Hall
37 Florence St., Malden, MA 02148
Second Sunday Except April, July &
    August, 9:00am
Bimonthly Newsletter, Biennial Roster
Annual Show, April
Cape Cod Post Card Collectors Club
Founded 1985
Sue Beyle, Pres.
P.O. Box 946, North Eastham, MA
    02651
PH: 508-255-3389
Helen Angell, Memb.
Short Neck Rd., So. Dennis, MA 02660

PH: 508-398-1793
Dues: $5.00
Carlton Hall
Old Bass River Rd., Dennis, MA
Last Thursday Except July, August &
    September, 6:30pm
Quarterly Newsletter
Annual Show, September
Marblehead Post Card Club
John Griffiths, Pres. & Memb.
67 Naugus Ave., Marblehead, MA
    01945
PH: 617-631-6678
St. Stephen's Methodist Church
67 Cornell Rd., Marblehead, MA 01945
First Tuesday, 7:00pm

MICHIGAN
Southwest Michigan Post Card Club
Founded 1976
Joy Miller, Pres.
3919 Hayes, Portage, MI 49081
PH: 616-327-8005
Stanley Smeed, Memb.
1419 Baker Dr., Kalamazoo, MI 49001
Dues: $2.00
Meeting Locations Vary, Call for
    Information
First Monday, 7:00pm
Annual Roster
2 Shows Per Year, April & October

Wolverine Postcard Club
Founded 1954
Christine Shurtieff, Pres.
20970 Hunt St., Roseville, MI 48066
PH: 313-777-7014
Laura Goldberg, Memb.
1313 E. Harry, Hazel Park, MI 48030
PH: 313-545-8552
Dues: $7.00, $1.00 Additional Family
    Members
Laura Goldberg Home
1313 E. Harry, Hazel Park, MI 48030
Second Saturday, 12:00noon
Quarterly Bulletin, Annual Roster

MINNESOTA
Twin City Postcard Club
Founded: 1970
Bob Stumm, Pres.
P.O. Box 2493, Minneapolis, MN 55402
David Johnson, Memb.
P.O. Box 2493, Minneapolis, MN 55402
PH: 612-426-3573
Dues: $8.00, $1.00 Each Additional
    Family Member
Richfield Community Center
70th St. & Nicollet Ave. S., Richfield,
    MN
Third Wednesday Except July &
    December, 6:30pm
Monthly Bulletin, Annual Roster
2 Shows Per Year, March & September

MISSOURI
Gateway Postcard Club
Founded 1974
Ray Steinnerd, Pres.
4474 Gemini Dr., St. Louis, MO 63128
Kathy Danielsen, Memb.
P.O. Box 630, O'Fallon, IL 62269
PH: 618-632-1921
Dues: $7.00
Kirkwood Community Center
111 Geyer Rd., Kirkwood, MO
First Monday Except September,
    7:30pm
Bimonthly Newsletter, Annual Roster
2 Shows Per Year, Spring & Fall
Heart of America Postcard Collectors,
Inc.
Founded 1982
D.E. Harmon, Pres.
P.O. Box 24690, Kansas City, MO 64131
PH: 913-268-6149
Warren Beach, Memb.
P.O. Box 24690, Kansas City, MO 64131
PH: 913-631-9111
Dues: $7.50
All Souls Unitarian Church
4500 Warwick, Kansas City, MO
Third Tuesday—February, March,
    April, September, October, Novem-
    ber, 7:00pm
Quarterly Newsletter, Annual Roster
Annual Show, May

NEBRASKA

Lincoln Postcard Club
Founded 1986
Robert H. 'Bob' Bauer, Pres.
8620 Old Cheney Rd., Lincoln, NE 68526
PH: 402-483-5796
Doug Roberts, Memb.
3440 Melrose Ave., Lincoln, NE 68506
PH: 402-488-4734
Dues: $6.00 Active, $5.00 Associate
Holiday Inn Northeast
5250 Cornhusker Hwy., Lincoln, NE
Third Thursday Except July & December, 7:30pm
Annual Roster, 10 Newsletters Per Year
Annual Show, Spring

NEW HAMPSHIRE

Granite State Postcard Collectors Club
Founded 1983
Gordan Root, Pres.
R.F.D. #1, Box 42B, Lancaster, NH 03584
Gladys Morabito, Memb.
P.O. Box 109, Rumney, NH 03266
Dues: $6.00, $12.00 Foreign
Unitarian Church
Central St., Franklin, NH 03235
Third Saturday, 9:00am
Monthly Newsletter, Quarterly Gazette, Yearly Roster
2 Shows Per Year, June & October

NEW JERSEY

Central Jersey Deltiological Society, Inc.
Founded 1981
Ginny Folger, Pres. & Memb.
215 E. High St., Apt. 2, Somerville, NJ 08876
PH: 201-725-0935
Knights Of Columbus Hall
Grove St. & South Ave., Dunellen, NJ 08812
Third Sunday, 1:00pm
Monthly Newsletter, Annual Roster, Quarterly Journal
Garden State Post Card Collectors Club
Joan Kay, Pres.
Dolores Kirchgessner, Memb.
421 Washington St., Hoboken, NJ 07030
PH: 201-659-1922
Dues: $5.00, $4.00 Additional Members
Elks Club
70 Springfield Ave., Springfield, NJ
First Sunday Except October, 11:30am
Periodic Newsletter, Annual Roster
Annual Show, October
South Jersey Post Card Club
Founded 1971
David B. Grubbs, Pres.
212 Kathy Dr., Yardley, PA 18067
Alex Antal, Memb.
#4 Plymouth Dr., Marlton, NJ 08053
PH: 609-983-1450

Dues: $6.00, $9.00 Family
Holiday Inn
Runnemede, NJ
Fourth Sunday Except April, 1:00pm
Quarterly Bulletin, Monthly Newsletter, Roster $1.00
Annual Show, April

NEW YORK

Buffalo Postcard Club
Harvey Holzworth, Pres.
186 Sterling Ave., Buffalo, NY 14216
Ken Butts, Memb.
97 Fairhaven Dr., Cheektowaga, NY 14225
PH: 716-634-5970
Dues: $7.00 First Year, $5.00 Thereafter
Cleveland Heights Christian Church
4774 Union Rd., Cheektowaga, NY 14225
First Tuesday, 7:00pm
Annual Show, March
Central New York Post Card Club
Sandra J. Drake, Pres.
R.D.2, Box 144, Canastota, NY 13032
Ruth R. Weimer, Memb.
R.D.2, Box 173, RTE. 31, Canastota, NY 13032
PH: 315-697-7157
Dues: $8.00
Various Towns
Quarterly Bulletin, Annual Roster
2 Shows Per Year, April & September

Corning-Painted Post Postcard Society
Founded 1977
Gertrude Boland, Pres. & Memb.
136 High Rd., Corning, NY 14830
Dues: None
Public Library
Nasser Plaza, Corning, NY 14830
Second Thursday, 7:00pm

Kaaterskill Post Card Club, Inc.
Founded 1975
Donald Stephens, Pres.
P.O. Box 177, Glenford, NY 12433
PH: 914-657-2153
Eric Fedde, Memb.
Rd. 1 Box 418A, Stone Ridge, NY 12484
PH: 914-687-7555
Dues: $5.00, $6.00 Family, $10.00
    Foreign
Hurley Reformed Church
Main St., Hurley, NY
First Wednesday, 7:30pm
Monthly Newsletter, Annual Roster
3 Shows Per Year

Long Island Postcard Club
Gary Hammond, Pres.
Eric Karlson, Memb.
2455 Union Blvd., Apt. 4K, Islip, NY
    11751
PH: 516-581-0465
Dues: $7.00, $10.00 Family
Good Shepherd Lutheran Church
Hempstead Turnpike, Levittown, NY

First Thursday Except July & August,
    6:30pm
Quarterly Bulletin, Annual Roster
Annual Show, Spring

Metropolitan Post Card Club
Founded 1946
Leah Schnall, Pres.
67-00 192nd St., Flushing, NY 11365
PH: 718-454-1272
Rae Schnall, Memb.
67-00 192nd St., Flushing, NY 11365
PH: 718-454-1272
Dues: $10.00
Days Inn
440 W. 57th St., New York, NY 10019
Second Sunday Except May & Novem-
    ber, 10:00am
Bimonthly Newsletter, Biennial Roster
2 Shows Per Year, May & November

Post Card Club Of Oswego County
Founded 1981
Roseanne Costello, Pres.
216 E. 9th St., Oswego, NY 13126
PH: 315-342-0388
Lillian McCloskey, Memb.
7 West 8th St., Oswego, NY 13126
PH: 315-343-1049
Dues: $3.00, $5.00 Family
Roy McCrobie Bldg.
Lake St., Oswego, NY 13126
Second Wednesday, Oct-June, 7:00pm
2 Newsletters Per Year, Annual Show

Upstate New York Post Card Club
Founded 1972
James Davis, Pres.
5 Cutter Dr., Johnstown, NY 12095
PH: 518-762-8659
Dorothy Baron, Memb.
1832 Fiero Ave., Schenectady, NY 12303
PH: 518-355-5885
Dues: $4.00
Second Presbyterian Church
25 Church St., Amsterdam, NY 12010
Second Friday Except July & Septem-
    ber, 7:00pm
Annual Roster, 6 Bulletins Per Year
Annual Show, September

Western New York Postcard Club
Founded 1975
John Williams, Pres.
7217 Lake Ave., Williamson, NY 14589
PH: 315-589-8400
Jane Schryver, Memb.
226 Main St., Dansville, NY 14437-1112
PH: 716-335-3121
Dues: $8.00, $10.00 Family
Carmen Clark Lodge
Brighton Town Park, 777 Westfall Rd.,
    Rochester, NY 14618
Second Saturday or Sunday Except
    December (call for day), 12:00 Noon
Bimonthly Bulletin, 5 Newsletters Per
    Year, Annual Roster
Annual Show, October

NORTH CAROLINA

Tarheel Postcard Club
Founded 1978
Russ Southworth, Pres.
2405 Pineview Dr., Greensboro, NC
27407
PH: 919-299-5262
Roberta Greiner, Memb.
1614 Helmwood Dr., Greensboro, NC
27410
PH: 919-852-3495
Dues: $3.00, $5.00 Family
Secretary's Home
1614 Helmwood Dr., Greensboro, NC
27410
Floating Saturdays Except July &
August, 1:00pm
Annual Roster, 10 Newsletters Per Year

OHIO

Greater Cincinnati Post Card Club
Founded 1983
George Budd, Pres.
6910 Tenderfoot Lane, Cincinnati, OH
45249
PH: 513-489-0518
Al Wettstein, Memb.
23-90 8 Mile Rd., Cincinnati, OH 45244
Dues: $4.00
Brookwood Retirement Community
12100 Reed Hartman Hwy., Cincinnati,
OH 45241
Second Sunday Except June, July &
August, 2:00pm
Heart of Ohio Post Card Club
Founded 1975
Jim Davis, Pres.
2693 Alder Vista Dr., Columbus, OH
43221
PH: 614-891-0020
Mrs. P.H. George, Memb.
1701 East Cooke Rd., Columbus, OH
43224-2110
PH: 614-268-7622
Dues: $5.00, $7.50 Couple
Chemical Abstract
Olentangy River Rd., Columbus, OH
Second Thursday, 7:00pm
Quarterly Newsletter, Annual Roster
Three Shows Per Year
Johnny Appleseed Postcard Club, Inc.
James Perkins, Pres.
1023 Cooper Dr., Ashland, OH 44805
Mabelle Perkins, Memb.
1023 Cooper Dr., Ashland, OH 44805
PH: 419-289-2467, 419-289-6607
Dues: $5.00, $7.50 Family
Pic-A-Deli Restaurant
4 East Main St., Ashland, OH 44805
First Monday Except January &
February, 7:00pm
10 Newsletters Per Year
Annual Show, June
Tri-County Postcard Club
Founded 1990
Ray Ferrell, Pres. & Memb.
332 St. Clair Ave., Cadiz, OH 43907

PH: 614-942-3475
Dues: $5.00
Buckeye House Apartments
201 E. 3rd, Uhrichsville, OH 44683
Second Monday, 7:00pm
Western Reserve Post Card Society
Founded 1973
Paul Knapp, Pres.
25028 Rainbow Dr., Olmsted Falls, OH
44138
PH: 216-234-4441
Shirley Goldberg, Memb.
2673 Cranlyn Rd., Cleveland, OH 44122
Dues: $7.00
Airport Ramada Inn
16501 Brookpark Rd., Cleveland, OH
Third Saturday Except July & August,
10:00am
8 Newsletters Per Year, Biennial Roster
Annual Show, May

OKLAHOMA

T-Town Postcard Club
Founded 1981
David Reeh, Pres.
Lavoy Hatchett, Memb.
P.O. Box 906116, Tulsa, OK 74112
PH: 918-743-1854
Dues: $6.00, $1.00 Additional Family
Members
Eastland Mall Community Center
145th East Ave. & 21st St., Tulsa, OK
First Tuesday, 7:00pm
10 Newsletters Per Year, Annual Roster
Annual Show

OREGON

Southern Oregon Philatelic Society
Larry Crain, Pres.
807 Pennsylvania, Medford, OR 97501
Elsie Sterton, Memb.
59 Summit, Medford, OR 97501
PH: 503-772-7209
B.L.M. Building
3040 Biddle Rd., Medford, OR 97501
First Thursday, 7:30pm
2 Shows Per Year, April & October
Webfooters Post Card Club
Founded 1966
Charles Gillespie, Pres.
P.O. Box 13145, Portland, OR 97213
Mona I. Campbell, Memb.
13025 S.W. Grant Ave., Tigard, OR
97223-5101
PH: 503-639-1507
Dues: $7.00, $7.50 Family
Holgate House
4601 S.E. 39, Portland, OR
Third Weekend, Alternate Days, 12:00
Noon
Quarterly Bulletin, Annual Roster
Annual Shows

PENNSYLVANIA

Anthracite Postcard Club
Founded 1987
Norm Brauer, Pres.

114 W. Main St., Dalton, PA 18414
Connie Horn, Memb.
Box 102 Rd. #1, New Milford, PA 18834
Dues: $5.00
Clarks Summit Boro Hall
Clarks Summit, PA 18411
Second Sunday Except Summer,
7:00pm
Bimonthly Newsletter, Annual Roster

Greater Johnstown Postcard Club
Founded 1982
Ken Beaner, Pres.
1011 Linton St., Johnstown, PA 15905
PH: 814-536-4082
Carole Barto, Memb.
1097-1/2 Edson Ave., Johnstown, PA
15905
PH: 814-535-2369
Dues: $5.00, $8.00 Family
First United Federal Bldg., Community
Room
227 Franklin St., Johnstown, PA
Third Thursday Except August &
December, 7:00pm
Annual Roster
Lancaster County Postcard Club
Founded 1990
Earl Carver, Pres.
212 Pheasant Dr., Columbia, PA 17512
PH: 717-684-3069
Dorathy Fry, Memb.
1050 Kleinfelterville Rd., Stevens, PA
17578
PH: 717-733-8918
Dues: $7.00, $10.00 Family
Manheim Twp. Municipal Bldg.
1821 Municipal Dr., Lancaster, PA
Third Monday, 7:00pm
Monthly Newsletter

Lehigh Valley Post Card Club
Founded 1983
M. Gene Mickel, Pres.
201 Prospect St., Delaware Park,
Phillipsburg, NJ 08865-1342
PH: 201-859-4242
R.F. Kichline, Memb.
P.O. Box 3008, Palmer, PA 18043
Dues: $5.00, $7.00 Family
2nd National Bank Of Nazareth,
Newburg Branch
Rt. 191 & Newburg Rd., Nazareth, PA
Third Tuesday, 6:30pm
Monthly Newsletter Except December,
Annual Roster
Annual Show, October
Morlatton Postcard Club
Founded 1975
Myrta Hall, Pres.
Lane, SC 29564
PH: 803-387-6062
Anne Darrah, Memb.
528 W. Baumstown Rd., Birdsboro, PA
19508
PH: 215-582-4810
Dues: $4.00, $5.00 Family
2 Shows Per Year, Spring & Fall
Postcard Collector Annual

Pocono Postcard Collectors Club
Bob Kaiser, Pres.
Emily Carter, Memb.
279 Locust Ridge Rd., Pocono Lake, PA
    18347
PH: 717-646-2879
Dues: $3.00
Delaware Water Gap Methodist Church
Delaware Water Gap, PA 18327
Third Saturday, 7:30pm
Monthly Newsletter
2 Shows Per Year

Susquehanna Valley Postcard Club
Founded 1982
Roy Shoop, Pres.
P.O. Box 132, Northumberland, PA
    17857
Ralph Vanderbeck, Memb.
P.O. Box 132, Northumberland, PA
    17857
Dues: $5.00, $1.00 Additional Family
    Members
Hunter Mansion Museum
N. Front St. (Rear), Sunbury, PA
Last Sunday, 6:00pm
Monthly Newsletter, Annual Roster
Annual Show, June

3 Rivers Postcard Club
George Smurlo, Pres.
Alan Stricker, Memb.
3025 Washington Rd., McMurray, PA
    15317
Dues: $6.00
Mt. Lebanon Methodist Church
3319 W. Liberty Ave., Mt. Lebanon, PA
Third Wednesday, 7:30pm
Monthly Newsletter, Annual Roster

**Washington Crossing Card Collectors
    Club**
Founded 1972
Vernon Wersler, Pres.
P.O. Box 39, Washington Crossing, PA
    18977
PH: 215-345-0408
David Grubbs, Memb.
P.O. Box 39, Washington Crossing, PA
    18977
PH: 215-493-0618
Dues: $5.00, $7.00 Family
Titusville Presbyterian Church
River Rd., Titusville, NJ 08560
Second Monday, 8:00pm
Monthly Bulletin, Annual Roster

York Post Card Club
Founded 1989
Kenneth McClain, Pres.
P.O. Box 173, York, PA 17405-0173
PH: 717-764-6319
Richard Bishop, Memb.
P.O. Box 173, York, PA 17405-0173
Dues: $5.00
United Way Bldg.
800 E. King St., York PA 17402
Second Monday, 7:00pm

RHODE ISLAND
Rhode Island Post Card Club
Founded 1958
Raymond A. Zwolenski, Pres.
71 Boardman Ave., Cumberland, RI
    02864
PH: 401-658-2812
Evelyn M. Marshall, Memb.
37 Ryder Ave., Apt. 2, Cranston, RI
    02920-5409
Dues: $9.00
Knights Of Columbus Building
1 New Road, Rumford, RI
Last Sunday Except July And August,
    8:00am
Bimonthly Bulletin Except July/
    August, Biannual Roster
Annual Show, October

TENNESSEE
East Tennessee Postcard Club
Founded 1989
Milton Hinshilwood, Pres.
523 Morrell Rd. D-52, Knoxville, TN
    37919
PH: 615-693-4313
Elena I. Zimmerman, Memb.
7914 Gleason Dr. #1061, Knoxville, TN
    37919
PH: 615-690-6469
Dues: $5.00
Clubhouse
7914 Gleason Dr., Knoxville, TN 37919
Fourth Saturday, 11:00am
Annual Roster

TEXAS
Borderland Postcard Club
Mary Sarber, Pres. & Memb.
1024 Oneida, El Paso, TX 79912
PH: 915-581-0950
Dues: $5.00
El Paso Public Library
501 N. Oregon, El Paso, TX
Second Tuesday, 7:00pm
Occasional Newsletter, Roster Available
    Upon Request
Annual Show
Capital Of Texas Post Card Club
Founded 1990
Robert Fesler, Pres.
P.O. Box 202471, Austin, TX 78720
PH: 512-260-2630
Kathy Fesler, Memb.
P.O. Box 202471, Austin, TX 78720
PH: 512-260-2630
Dues: $8.00, $1.00 Additional Family
    Members
Windows To The Past
5525 Burnet Ave., Austin, TX 78756
Second Sunday, 2:00pm
Quarterly Bulletin
Cowtown Post Card Club
Founded 1956
Millie Poledna, Pres.
7504 Madeira, Fort Worth, TX 76111
PH: 817-451-3930
Ruth Scott, Memb.

1615 Bluebonnet Dr., Fort Worth, TX
    76111
PH: 817-834-0103
Dues: $6.00, $1.00 Per Additional
    Family Members
Members' Homes
Third Sunday, 2:00pm
Monthly Newsletter, Annual Roster
Annual Show, Third Weekend in
    August
Dallas Metroplex Postcard Club
Founded 1983
Leroy King, Jr., Pres.
4815 Allencrest, Dallas, TX 75244
PH: 214-239-1280
Larry W. Seymour, Memb.
822 SE 8th St., Grand Prairie, TX 75051
PH: 214-264-0723
Dues: $6.00
Farmers Branch Manske Library
13613 Webb Chapel, Farmers Branch,
    TX 75234
Saturday, 1:00pm
Annual Roster, Monthly Bulletin
Annual Show, March
Greater Houston Postcard Society
Debbie Hart, Pres.
8502 Woodcamp, Houston, TX 77088
PH: 713-999-3936
Mary Chapman, Memb.
4816 Palmetto, Bellaire, TX 77401
PH: 713-461-1374
Dues: $6.00, $2.50 Additional Family
    Members, $7.50 Foreign
Tides II Motor Inn
6700 S. Main, Houston, TX
First Thursday Except Summer, 7:00pm
Quarterly Newsletter, Annual Roster
Annual Show, October
Houston Post Card Club
Founded 1977
Genevieve Williams, Pres.
2700 Bellefontaine, #A-4, Houston, TX
    77025
PH: 713-664-2823
Gloria Grolla, Memb.
1616 Park Haven, Houston, TX 77077
PH: 713-589-1873
Dues: $6.00, $7.00 Family, $3.00 Junior
Wyatt's Cafeteria
Sharpstown Mall, Houston, TX
Third Sunday, 2:00pm
Quarterly Newsletter, Annual Roster
Annual Show, March

UTAH
Utah Postcard Collectors Club
Founded 1986
Dennis Goreham, Pres. & Memb.
1539 East 4070 South, Salt Lake City,
    UT 84124
PH: 801-277-5119
Stan Sander's Bottle Museum
2743 South Blair St. (360 East), Salt Lake
    City, UT
Fourth Thursday, 7:00pm
Monthly Newsletter

VIRGINIA

Old Dominion Postcard Club
Founded 1978
Jim Adams, Pres.
8611 Beacontree Ln., #4, Richmond, VA 23229
PH: 804-346-4938
Sharon Benenson, Memb.
3002 Gay Ave., Richmond, VA 23231
PH: 804-236-8811
Dues: $8.00, $10.00 Family
Signet Bank Bldg.
N. 8th & E. Main St., Richmond, VA 23219
Second Tuesday, 7:00pm
Annual Show, November

Postcard History Society
Founded 1975
John McClintock, Dir.
P.O. Box 1765, Manassas, VA 22110
PH: 703-368-2757
Dues: $5.00
Manassas School Of Dance, Manassas Shopping Center
Mathis Ave., Manassas, VA
Third Sunday Except July, August, September, 1:00pm
Quarterly Bulletin
2 Shows Per Year

WASHINGTON

Pacific Northwest Post Card Club
Robert Norton, Pres.
Rich Klepac, Memb.
28828 207th S.E., Kent, WA 98042
PH: 206-630-2012
Dues: $6.00, $9.00 Canada, $17.00 Foreign
Lake City Community Center
12531 28th Ave. NE, Seattle, WA 98125
First Sunday Except July & August, 12:00noon
Bimonthly Bulletin, Annual Roster

WISCONSIN

Four Lakes Postcard Club
Founded 1988
Joe Stransky, Pres.
209 Ramsey Court, Madison, WI 53704
PH: 608-249-4875
Ann Waidelich, Memb.
2150 Lakeland Ave., Madison, WI 53704
PH: 608-249-7920
Dues: $3.00
Wil-Mar Neighborhood Center
953 Jenifer St., Madison, WI 53703
Fourth Tuesday, 7:30pm
Newsletter, Annual Roster
Annual Show, January

Milwaukee Post Card Collectors Club
Robert Koehler, Pres.
P.O. Box 10153, Milwaukee, WI 53210
PH: 414-442-4700
John Ford, Memb.
P.O. Box 10153, Milwaukee, WI 53210
Dues: $5.00
Forest Home Library
1432 W. Forest Home Ave., Milwaukee, WI
First Monday, 7:00pm
Quarterly Newsletter, Annual Roster
2 Shows Per Year, April & October

CANADA

Golden Horseshoe Post Card Club
Paul McWhinnie, Pres.
Louise Kaye, Memb.
P.O. Box 4201 Stn. D, Hamilton, Ontario, Canada L8V 4L6
Dues: $5.00, $1.00 Each Additional Family Member
Burlington Spectator Bldg.
534 Brant St., Burlington, Ontario, Canada
Fourth Wednesday Except July, August, December, 7:30pm
Annual Roster, 3 Newsletters Per Year
Annual Show

Toronto Postcard Club
Founded 1977
Wilf Cowin, Pres.
P.O. Box 6184, Postal Station A, Toronto, Ontario, Canada M5W 1P6
Dave Card, Memb.
P.O. Box 6184, Postal Station A Toronto, Ontario, Canada M5W 1P6
Dues: $15.00, $20.00 U.S., $25.00 Foreign
Agincourt Collegiate Institute, Room 113
Midland Ave., Scarborough, Ontario, Canada
2nd & 4th Thursday Except July & August & 4th Thursday June & December, 8:00pm
3 Newsletters/Year, Annual Roster
Annual Show, Last Sunday in February

Vancouver Post Card Club
Founded 1980
Don Steele, Pres.
1840 Orchard Way, West Vancouver, BC, Canada V7V 4G2
PH: 604-922-9688
Elizabeth Meyers, Memb.
1415 East 13th Ave., Vancouver, BC, Canada V5N 2B5
PH: 604-874-2710
Dues: $12.00

Hastings Community Center
3096 East Hastings St., Vancouver, BC, Canada V5K 2A3
Third Tuesday Except July & August, 7:00pm
Bimonthly Newsletter
Annual Show

MAIL CLUBS

Cosmopolitan Post Card Club
Frank Pichardo, Memb.
P.O. Box 1116, Flushing, NY 11354
PH: 718-359-1183
Dues: $15.00/Two Years
Annual Roster, 8 Bulletins Per Year

Ephemera Society Of America, Inc.
WM. Frost Mobley, Pres.
P.O. Box 10, Schoharie, NY 12157
Mary McCabe, Memb.
P.O. Box 224, Ravena, NY 12143
PH: 518-756-6216

Garfield Gang Post Card Club
Founded 1986
Joan B. Carlson, Pres. & Memb.
905 Route 163, Oakdale, CT 06370
Dues: $3.00
Quarterly Newsletter, Auction

Horse Collectors Of America
Founded 1987
Miriam Hall, Pres. & Memb.
4015 Kandy Dr., Austin, TX 78749
Dues: $7.00
Annual Roster, 4 Newsletters Per Year

International Disney Post Card Collectors Club
Founded 1987
Jay Patel, Memb.
2500 Battleground Ave., Greensboro, NC 27408
Dues: $4.00, $5.00 Canada, $6.00 Foreign
Quarterly Newsletter, Annual Roster

Maximum Card Study Unit
Sebastian Safiano, V. Pres.
9046 S.W. 112 Court, Miami, FL 33176
PH: 305-271-7788
Ed Cramer, Memb.
4702 D Main St., Skokie, IL 60076
PH: 708-679-7356
Dues: $7.00, $12.00 Foreign
Quarterly Newsletter

Organization For Collectors of Covered Bridge Postcards
Kay Lloyd, Pres.
7 Squantum St., Milton, MA 02186
Linda Jane Willauer, Memb.
110 Shady Lane, Fayetteville, NY 13066
Dues: $4.00
Bimonthly Bulletin, Annual Roster

Collecting Modern Postcards

By Dave Long

In the June 1990 issue of *Postcard Collector* (pages 8-10), my entire column was devoted to "Why Collect Modern Postcards?" For those who missed this piece and because the modern postcard era covers such a lengthy period and wide variety of subjects, it's important that it once again be covered.

Moderns have been around for many years. They first appeared in the U.S. back in 1939 with the introduction of a standard size chrome series of Union Oil advertising postcards. The series was a travelog of sorts, featuring attractions in western states on the picture side and mention of Union Oil on the reverse side. Additional Union Oil series were produced annually until about 1946-47. By 1950 the modern chrome postcard was here to stay. It had effectively replaced its linen predecessor.

Before continuing, it should be pointed out that chrome is not synonymous with modern. It's true that all chromes are moderns, but not true that all moderns are chromes. Some moderns are printed with a flat, linen-like finish, while others are more like a real photo. Other variations also exist. So, for the purpose of this column, "modern" refers to the era and not its product. And for those unfamiliar with the term "chrome," it refers to the sort of postcard offered on today's card racks—full-color, glossy finish.

In general, the first chromes produced were the 3-1/2"x5-1/2" standard size cards. From their introduction until the mid to late 1970s, the standard size chrome was the mainstay of the industry and favorite of the modern collector. By the early 1980s, however, the present day 4"x6" continental had made significant inroads. An educated guess would put current postcard production at 60-70 percent continental, 10 percent standard size, and the remaining 20-30 percent in larger or odd-sized cards. While many current collectors prefer the standard size card because it's easy to file, most readily accept the continental. With some exceptions, chiefly cheesecake, dated events, and stadiums, oversize and odd-sized cards are unacceptable as collectibles.

In it's infancy, the chrome seemed an incredible improvement over the flat-finished linen. It was a brand new innovation, complete with a more vibrant color and sleek finish. Those factors alone gave it more collectible appeal than the subject it pictured. Since those early days, the chrome has only gotten better. The combination of excellent photography, graphic possibilities, the very latest in printing techniques, and an unlimited supply of material to photograph have all helped to make today's postcard a terrific product with great collector appeal. Intense competition from the very first has also had much to do with the way today's cards look. In the early days of the chrome, prominent printing firms included such names as Curt Teich, Dexter Press, H.S. Crocker, Koppel, Mike Roberts, Plastichrome, and Tichnor Bros. Practically 100 percent of the early chromes were made in the U.S.; most by these few firms, many of which have since been purchased by other firms or gone out of business. Curt Teich and Plastichrome cards are being produced in Ireland by John Hinde. Dexter Press was purchased by H.S. Crocker, which is now owned by a Canadian firm. Mike Roberts remains active, but on a limited basis. Koppel and Tichnor Bros. no longer exist. While other U.S. postcard printing firms are active, a large share of current production is by overseas firms, primarily Asian and European. In general, their postcards are excellent.

Now that I've provided a bit of general background information pertaining to the modern era, I want to cover some of the specifics it has to offer the collector, including reasons for collecting, what is available, popular topics to collect, and developing trends. I'll also offer a few hints that may help your collecting become more enjoyable.

#CT-3173, Smith-Western Co. Death Valley. Good example of blended border w/special graphics. Could this be the first of a new trend?

Why Collect Moderns?

Since its period covers 40-plus years, a longer time span than for any of its predecessors, the modern era suggests the very same reasons for collecting its cards as for those of any other period, even nostalgia. The period offers a pictorial documentation of everything that's taken place since 1950, including changes in our communities, social and political history, modes of dress, transportation, advertising, humor, disasters, military, people in general, and anything else you can mention, including our pastimes. Much of this material is available only on moderns. Two good examples are Disney and space. They simply don't exist on older cards. Besides the various reasons for collecting moderns because of their content, there are other reasons equally viable. There is the enjoyment factor. Simply put, they're fun to collect. In general, they're of good to excellent quality, reasonably priced, and readily available. In contrast to the collectors of older postcards, many modern collectors are actively involved amongst themselves with postcard exchanges by mail in the form of personal trades or round robins. Thus, there is also the factor of sharing ones hobby and collecting interests directly with other collectors.

What is Available?

I'd estimate there are a minimum of 400 view card distributors located throughout the U.S. Some are small "mom and pop" operations covering a very limited geographic area. Others are huge "regional" operations covering enormous territories. For example, White House covers the city of Cincinnati and a few select subjects across the Ohio River in

#P7290, Argus Communications. Garfield. Example of greetings/humor. There are many Garfield collectors.

Kentucky. On the other hand, Smith-Western and Smith-Southwestern Inc. (all part of one huge firm) cover all of Washington, Oregon, California, Arizona, and New Mexico, plus portions of Nevada, Utah, Colorado, and Texas. Some distributors offer a blanket-coverage of worthy subjects in their coverage area while others prefer to single out more specific attributes. A good example is the state of Kansas, which is covered by three very good distributors. Avery Postcards and the Dunlap Postcard Co. both offer large lines covering the cities and towns, historical sites, tourist attractions, and prominent physical features. The Kansas Postcard Co., on the other hand, has chosen to

limit it's line to the Lawrence/Topeka areas, plus a variety of general Kansas scenes including fields, streams, stone fences, wildlife, Indians, etc. With so many distributors offering such a wide array of subject matter, each in their own approach, there simply isn't space for more discussion at this point.

Each of the aforementioned types of distributors has its postcard line printed for them by one or more printing firms such as Crocker, McGrew, Mike Roberts, etc., or any of the numerous foreign printers. In this sense, then, the printers are actually contract printers or job printers, who print postcards exclusively for those distributors who contract jobs with them. Some printers also offer their own line of stock cards which are available to any distributor who wants them. Such stock lines are rather general in nature and may include generic landscapes, domestic and wild animals, greetings, etc. In the heyday of the standard size chrome, several printers also offered state maps and capitols as a part of their stock line. These are favorite collectibles today. A rather specialized line of stock cards is being printed today by H.S. Crocker—Disney productions for distribution outside the theme parks, specifically in the states of California and Florida or in general elsewhere. Crocker also prints additional Disney cards for distribution within the theme parks and for specific distributors such as Luna Bay Productions.

Besides the view card distributors, there exists an unknown number of specialized modern distributors of topicals. Most cards are offered on a chrome stock, but many are printed on a flat or linen-like stock. A great many cards are printed

#MWP-SF15, Great Mountain West Supply. Transportation of sorts. Multiview w/key-line and color title bar running through black border.

in black & white or sepia, which is in contrast to the nearly 100 percent of view cards being printed in full color. Some of the better known specialized distributors include such firms as American Postcard Co., Azusa, Classico San Francisco, The Laughin' Place, Ludlow Sales (now a part of Classico), Dover Publications, Art Unlimited, Hallmark Cards, Athena, Pomegranate, Out of the West Publications, Mary Jayne's Railroad Specialties, Audio Visual, Argus Communications, and a whole raft of others. The U.S. is blessed with quite a number of these specialized firms, but the fact remains that the majority are based overseas, principally in Western Europe.

Subject matter offered by the specialized distributors is as varied as it is with the view card distributors. Looking at a few of them will give an idea of their coverage scope. Azusa offers a sizeable line of Indian photos printed in brown sepia—repros of famous photographers' works from the late 1800s to early 1900s. Classico San Francisco has a large line which includes movie, TV, and other personalities, Betty Boop, Norman Rockwell, Disney, art by Stephen Haines Hall and Leroy Neiman, plus much more. Their Ludlow Sales line is a very large one of primarily notable entertainers, printed in brown sepia. Audio Visual, Mary Jayne's, and other similar firms offer comprehensive lines of trains and planes. Dover Publications' line includes a wide variety of art, in both cut form and in postcard books. They've also issued numerous nostalgic postcard books featuring the way some of our larger cities looked in the early 1900s. Out of the West has published impressive lines of California and Florida crate label art plus a 60-card set of "Touring America," which features early automobile advertising art work. Humor is prevalent in the lines of Argus, Hallmark Cards, American Postcard, Argus, The Laughin' Place, and others. Pomegranate, Art Unlimited, Fotofolio,

#RS 1108, Schellmark, Inc. Hot air balloons, a popular category.

and Athena have diverse lines which include art, celebrities, nostalgia, novelty, erotica, some event documentation, and much more. Many of their cards are printed in black and white.

In addition to the myriad of modern postcards published by view card and specialty firms, countless others are issued by individuals, organizations and other small firms. Collectively, such publishers issue some of the best material available pertaining to advertising, causes, commemoratives, documentation of political and other events, humor, satire, etc.

So to specifically answer the question as to what's available in moderns—anything! It comes in a wide variety of styles and sizes and, for the most part, is plentiful in supply. It is there for the picking, and there's something for everyone.

Popular Collectible Topics

Ask any modern collector, and you'll find they generally seek numerous categories. Some are general collectors who collect most anything, while others collect specific subjects. Whatever the case, there are far too many possibilities for all to be listed in this article. Instead, I'll list some of the ones experiencing current popularity. And, in some cases, I'll offer some specific examples.

Some rather general collectible fields include U.S., foreign, specific states, cities

and towns, national parks and monuments, mountains, sunrises and sunsets, flowers, waterscapes, and the like. More specific topicals might include any of the following: aerial views, advertising (McDonald's), art, buildings (in general, public, by specific architect, etc.), cats, celebrities (from public, political, or entertainment segments), courthouses, covered bridges, current or dated events (political, entertainment, commemorative, disasters, etc.), dogs (typically specific breeds), dolls, fireworks, grist and windmills, homes/mansions, horses, hot air balloons, large letter lighthouses, lightning, main streets, military (personnel, bases, and equipment, especially planes, tanks, and ships), Olympics, people, pinups/nudes, political, rainbows, recipes, skylines, skyscrapers, space, stadiums, state cards (capitols, maps, flags, flowers, birds, etc.), transportation (in general, or specifically autos, trucks, motorcycles, river boats, Great Lakes shipping, cruise liners, military ships/boats, railroads/trams/trollies, and anything else that moves), work-related/occupations, World's Fairs, and more. Some collectors want moderns in sets. Others are rather general collectors who are guided by style or size—standard size only, full-bleed, colored borders, no printing on the picture, etc. And, there are collectors who collect specific publishers or printers by stock number, regardless of the subjects depicted. Mike Roberts is one such firm whose cards are eagerly sought by many.

Developing Trends

Briefly, the quality of modern postcards is generally excellent and will continue to improve in the future. The flurry of activity with colored borders and other highlighted graphics appears here to stay, but will be interspersed with full-bleed images. Although of very limited interest to collectors, the oversize cards (larger than continental) will continue to capture a larger share of the view card market-

Left: #105-126, Classico San Francisco, Inc. Spock and Captain Kirk from Star Trek®. Example of celebrities from popular TV series. Right: #CT-440A, Smith-Western Co. Dated commemorative. Seattle's Lake Washington floating bridge, which sank on November 25, 1990.

place. As a result of consumer interest, or simply because the market hasn't been tapped, there will continue to be an infusion of the non-view card firms and all they have to offer. The outlook for modern postcards looks brighter than ever in the past and, since they're ephemeral in nature, now is a great time to collect them if you haven't already started!

In closing I'll offer a couple of tips. Even though moderns are relatively inexpensive and readily available, seek out good copies. Avoid dog-eared, worn cards.

Take care to see that your collection is securely housed. File boxes or drawers are fine, but don't pack your cards too tightly. If sleeves or albums are used, check periodically to make sure your moderns aren't bonding to the plastic. Be aware. This can happen with disastrous results. Lastly, find a filing and recording system that works for you. Checklists can be helpful. And it goes without saying that you should keep alert to what's happening with moderns through reading and your own explorations.

About the Author

Dave Long has collected postcards since 1949 and from the very first has specialized in moderns. For the past 7-1/2 years he has sold modern postcards to collectors; since July 1989 with Diane Allmen under the name Modern Postcard Sales. Since the first issue of Postcard Collector, *he has authored the monthly column "Small Talk," which discusses findings and trends in the field of modern postcards as seen through his eyes.*

  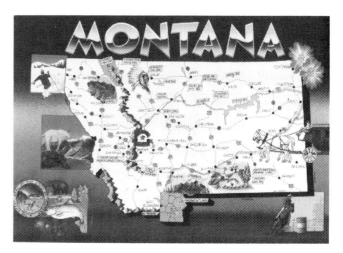

Left: #2USMA311, L.B. Prince, Inc. Political. Pres. Bush w/Presidential Seal. Right: No #, Seaich Corp. Montana state map w/insets of state seal, flower, etc. Popular category.

Dealer Directory

Dealers included in this directory are those who personally, or through their club, requested inclusion on the list and/or are members of the International Federation of Postcard Dealers (denoted with an * before their names). Dealers not included who wish to be named in the 1992 *Postcard Collector Annual* should send their information to the publisher.

ALABAMA

*Michael Smith
Ditto Falls Postcards
P.O. Box 12092
Huntsville, AL 35815
205-498-3834
Postcards, Paper Collectibles

ARIZONA

*Joan C. Angier
6365 W. Lost Canyon
Tucson, AZ 85745
602-743-7652
General Line

*Chas. W. Heckroth
Great Western Mails
P.O. Box 31510
Tucson, AZ 85751
602-296-1432

*Terry & Noreen Pavey
Verde Paper
P.O. Box 10614
Glendale, AZ 85318
602-439-2156
Postcards, Trade Cards, Arizona
    Documents

*Val Duane Robbins
Rimrock West
3450 North Drake Place
Tucson, AZ 85749
602-749-8774
General Line

ARKANSAS

*Tom & Mara Mertens
3605 Dunkeld Dr.
N. Little Rock, AR 72116
501-753-4254

CALIFORNIA

Michael Blessing
A.R.S.
24307 Majic Mtn. Pkwy., #124
Valencia, CA 91355
805-296-7586
Women, Nudes, Risque

Ralph Bowman
Paper Gallery
5349 Wheaton St.
La Mesa, CA 91942
619-462-6268
Topicals, States, Autographs
1991

Lee Brown
Adventure In Postcards
8423 Foothill Blvd.
Sunland, CA 91040
818-352-5663, 818-896-7919
Postcards, Paper Ephemera, Movie
    Material

*Gloria & Rudy Cazanjian
26920 Almaden Court
Los Altos Hills, CA 94022
415-941-1819
Children, Dolls, Toys

*Gordie's Used Cards
1235 Vista Superba
Glendale, CA 91205
818-246-6686

*Gisela Granstrom
4418 Dean Dr.
Ventura, CA 93003
805-642-0534

*Bill & Marilyn Hanson
P.O. Box 901
Ben Lomond, CA 95005-0901
408-336-5001
Better Views & Topicals

*Friedric Herbst
1055 Haight St.
San Francisco, CA 94117

Harold Holman
1212 Third St.
P.O. Box 416
Atwater, CA 95301
209-357-1373, 209-358-2671
Signed Artists, Old Postcards

*Vern Huffman
905 S. Idaho, #105
La Habra, CA 90631
213-690-4632

Joseph C. Jaynes
P.O. Box 1155
Santa Cruz, CA 95061
408-476-3262

*Roger LeRoque & Nick Farago
R & N Postcards
P.O. Box 217
Temple City, CA 91780
818-287-6066
West Coast Show Promoters

*Rita Nadler
Postcards Etc.
P.O. Box 4318
Thousand Oaks, CA 91359
Tucks, Louis Wain, Pioneers

Vic Pallos
658 Arden Ave.
Glendale, CA 91202
818-242-9055
Baseball Stadiums

*Ken Prag
Paper Americana
P.O. Box 531
Burlingame, CA 94011
415-566-6400
Quality Western State Views, Better
    Topicals, Stock Certificates & Bonds

*Rainbow's End Postcards
7 Comstock Rd.
Chico, CA 95928
916-893-2930

*Mike Rasmussen
Everything Paper
P.O. Box 726
Marina, CA 93933
408-384-5460
Postcards, Movie Memorabilia,
    Autographs

Jim Reid
J & K Postcards
P.O. Box 97
Carlsbad, CA 92018
619-431-0031
Real Photos, Western States, U.S.
    Military

*Pete Richards
Davis Gold & Silver Exchange
330 G St., Suite H
Davis, CA 95616
916-758-1334
Pre-1920 Western States, General
    Topicals

*Jerry Riley & Dorothy Whittaker
World Postcards
111 First St., Suite 15-978
Calexico, CA 92231
619-393-3929
Approvals, Appraisals

*Stephen T. Schmale
448 Tanglewood Court
Santa Rosa, CA 95409

Norm & Bess Sturgess
Inland Empire Postcards
360 W. 24th St.
San Bernardino, CA 92405
714-883-9075
Postcards, Advertising Cards

*Harry A. Victor
1408 18th Ave.
San Francisco, CA 94122
415-664-4286
Modern Limited Editions & British
    Royalty; Cigarette, Food & Beverage

COLORADO

Hope Firkins-Duncan
The Paper Lady
624 Pearl, #202
Boulder, CO 80302
303-442-0772
Colorado Small Towns, State Women,
    Signed Artists

*Ron Schwartz
3095-D South Peoria
Aurora, CO 80014
303-750-4695

CONNECTICUT

*William & Patricia Petersen
P.O. Box 398 (Summer)
Plainfield, CT 06374-0398
203-564-1494

*Jose L. Rodriguez
The Cartophilians
P.O. Box 903
430 Highland Ave.
Cheshire, CT 06410
203-272-2841, 203-272-1143
Postcards, Trade Cards, U.S. Postal
        History, Paper Americana
*Murray & Joanne Ruggiero
Ruggiero's
359 Silver Sands Rd.
East Haven, CT 06512-4125
203-469-7083
Worldwide, Want Lists, 100's of
        Categories
*Mary Ellen Seward
296 Palmer Hill Rd.
Riverside, CT 06878
*Marty, Jonah & Rita Shapiro
Postcards International
P.O. Box 2930
New Haven, CT 06515
203-865-0814
Mail Approvals, Picture Postcard
        Catalog, First National Postcard
        Auctions

DELAWARE
*Neal & Tillie Boyle
1545 Savannah Rd.
Lewes, DE 19958
302-645-7604

*Ken & Ginny Kolb
1117 Grinnell Rd.
Wilmington, DE 19803
302-478-6726
*Edward J. Masci
21 Hilton Rd.
Wilmington, DE 19810
302-475-8640

FLORIDA
*Theodore E. Bachman
6540 Baffin Dr. W.
Venice, FL 34293
813-497-6917
*Jim & Vera Berry
4100 E. Fletcher Ave.
Tampa, FL 33613
*Gladys Bruce
40 Sabal Palm Circle (Winter)
Eustis, FL 32726
*Edward M. Carter
P.O. Box 158
Boca Raton, FL 33429
*Christine's Collectible Cards
62 Sunset Rd.
Key Largo, FL 33037
305-852-8065
*Charles Croes & Ruth Brown
9261 S.W. 56th Terr.
Miami, FL 33273
305-274-9294

*Hank & Coby DeBoer
2 Aviles St.
St. Augustine, FL 32084
904-829-9673
*The Dekle's
707 32nd Ct.
Hollywood, FL 33021
305-981-6857
*Donald J. Gilluley
509 Lakeview St.
Orlando, FL 32804
407-839-1951
*Ed & Millie Goheen
The Goheens
6937 W. Camino Real
Boca Raton, FL 33433
305-392-2125
Alan F. Grab
Grab Bag Antiques, Inc.
10836 N.W. 30th Place (Winter)
Sunrise, FL 33322
305-572-4107
Quality Postcards, Paper Ephemera,
        Prints
*Halycon Hobbies
P.O. Box 561121
Miami, FL 33156
305-667-1117
*Henry Post Cards
12225 S.W. 24th Terr.
Miami, FL 33175
305-226-8296

*Bernice S. Kaufman
1239 S. Tamiami Trail
Sarasota, FL 33579
813-955-2625

*Clayton & Evelyn Keehn
Keehn Kollectibles
2117 Barcelona Dr.,
Clearwater, FL 34624
813-531-4807
Views, Sports, General Line

*Audrey K. Malone
1531 N. Drexel Rd.
Lot #409
West Palm Beach, FL 33417
407-687-3378
State Views, Detroit Publishing Co.,
   New York State

*Charles R. Mullen
2653 Grand Canyon St.
Sarasota, FL 34231
813-922-2246

*Marie H. Nemeth
35 Inglis Ave.
Inglis, FL 32649
904-447-2368

Larry Noder
P.O. Box 962
Odessa, FL 33556
813-960-9577
U.S. & German Military

*Robert Quay
Quay Postcards
K-12 Briny Breezes
Boynton Beach, FL 33435
407-276-9635

*Ellen W. Salander
61 N. Broadway
Englewood, FL 34223
813-474-4514

*Van R. Tippett
Tippett, Inc.
P.O. Box 49257
Sarasota, FL 34230
813-377-8886

*Michael B. Wasserberg
1025 Country Club Dr.
Margate, FL 33063
305-972-3789

*Eva U. Woodward
Jaywood
P.O. Box 375
Goldenrod, FL 32733
305-671-0559

GEORGIA

*J.C. Ballentine
Ballentines
P.O. Box 761
Hatcher Point Mall
Waycross, GA 31501
912-285-3250

Billy Horne
Mallard Nest Antiques
5860 Bankston Lake Rd.
Macon, GA 31206
912-788-8606
Blacks, Georgia

*Frank E. Howard
856 Charlotte St.
Macon, GA 31206
912-788-1514

*John A. Kovalski
43 Fountain Circle
Woodstock, GA 30188
404-255-7168

*Jack & Michael Leach
National Postcard Exchange
P.O. Box 886
225 Third St.
Macon, GA 31202-0886
912-743-8951
Rare Postcards, Common Postcards,
   General Line

*Ernest P. Malcom
Malcom Postcards
433 Plaza
Monroe, GA 30655
404-267-6897
General Line

*Charlie McCoy
Charlie's Cards
P.O. Box 516
180 Parkview Dr.
Commerce, GA 30529
404-335-3976
Buying Southern States, Views, Real
   Photos, Blacks

*Vickie & George Prater
Shiloh Postcards
P.O. Box 2004
Clayton, GA 30525
404-782-4100
Southern States, Wholesale Lots

*Carol Tuggle
The Gandy Dancer
5460 Peachtree Rd.
Chamblee, GA 30341
404-451-7425

ILLINOIS

Helen Ackert
521 S. 7th St.
DeKalb, IL 60115

Wayne F. Bauer
821 Winmore Dr.
Sleepy Hollow, IL 60118

*Danny & Kathy Danielsen
Metro East Promotions
P.O. Box 630
O'Fallon, IL 62269 (St. Louis area)
618-632-1921
Views, Greetings, Shop Sales

Stanley Dinsmore
5725 E. Pleasant St.
Belvidere, IL 61008
815-547-8771

Dorothy's Postcards
307 S. Euclid Ave.
Rockford, IL 61102
815-968-3959

Jennifer Henderson
Cookin' With Postcards
1744 W. Devon, Suite 23
Chicago, IL 60660
312-764-4428
Old & New Recipe Postcards

The Home Place Antiques
9633 Beaver Valley
Belvidere, IL 61008
815-547-5128

Jerry's Cards
2304 17th Ave.
Rockford, IL 61104
815-398-6380

Dwane Kaplenk
Rock Aires Postcards
P.O. Box 2301
Loves Park, IL 61131
815-398-0813

John W. Kuster
Yesteryear's Paper
102 Shady Lane Dr.
Dixon, IL 61021
815-288-2163
Riverboats, Railroad, Iowa-Illinois

*Robert H. Mangold
P.O. Box 295
Blue Island, IL 60406

*Ed McAllister
3413 W. Jefferson
Joliet, IL 60435
815-725-2504

Susan Nicholson
P.O. Box 595
Lisle, IL 60532
No View Cards

*Joan Quinones
386 33 Ave. Ct.
East Moline, IL 61244
309-755-9594
General Line, Paper Ephemera

*Ronald Reed
Reedson's
P.O. Box 935
Marion, IL 62959
618-993-5354

*J. Donald Schroth
P.O. Box 30
Clarendon Hills, IL 60514
312-323-3885

*Darlene & Wally Schultz
Remembered Treasures
230 N. Forest Court
Palatine, IL 60067
708-358-3226
Topicals, States, Foreign

John L. Simmons
John L. Simmons Postcards
P.O. Box 5044
Woodridge, IL 60517-1044
708-969-3215
Illinois Postal History, U.S. & Foreign

Fred Solberger
13006 N. Coon Rd.
Orangeville, IL 61060

*Norbert J. Stachura
P.O. Box 31005
Chicago, IL 60631
312-725-5123

Roy Strebing
3327 California Rd.
Rockford, IL 61108
815-226-8023

Rob Swanson
924 17th St.
Rockford, IL 61104
815-398-5384
*JoAnn & Bob Van Scotter
JoAnn Van Scotter Postcards
208 E. Lincoln St.
Mt. Morris, IL 61054
815-734-6971
Views, Transportation, Sports
*Arretta Wetzel
1325 45 St.
Rock Island, IL 61201
309-786-1335
Topicals, Greetings

INDIANA
*Douglas L. Acheson
Aladin Postcards
2801 E. Kessler Blvd.
Indianapolis, IN 46220
317-255-8379
Canada, Santas, Halloween
*Alan & Mary Christmas
P.O. Box 143
Lynnville, IN 47619
812-922-3654
Michael Collins
Rt. 2, Box 24
Hamilton, IN 46742
219-488-2003
Midwest Views, Real Photos
*Phil Collins
Rt. 4, Box 14
Floyds Knob, IN 47119
812-923-5326
Jerry & Sandi Garrett
Jerry's Antiques
1807 W. Madison St.
Kokomo, IN 46901
317-457-5256
Street Scenes
*Dave Long & Diane Allmen
Modern Postcard Sales
P.O. Box 644
Elkhart, IN 46515
219-264-0013
Modern Topicals, Chrome Views, All-
Era Price Guide
*Walter E. & Phyllis E. Mitchell
Walt & Phyl's Cards
611 Park Terrace
Columbia City, IN 46725-1949
219-244-4561
State Views, Topicals
Robert Pickard
M. & B. Hobbies
5010 W. 22nd St.
Indianapolis, IN 46224-5017
317-241-8777
Views, Courthouses, Transportation
Gerald Sanders
Antiques & Things
24 Fall St.
Williamsport, IN 47993
317-762-3687
Real Photos, U.S. Views, Signed Artists

*Jack & Vicki Stock
Retro-Spection
7850 Camelback Dr.
Indianapolis, IN 46250
317-841-7342
Rare & Unusual, Quality Greetings,
Topicals
*Anthony C. Turner
P.O. Box 905
Goshen, IN 46526
219-534-3015
Rick Weaver & Catherine Durbin
120 W. N. A St.
Gas City, IN 46933
317-674-2574
Santas, Street Scenes, Halloween
*S.G. 'Chic' Williams
Chic's Sale
5915 E. 12th St.
Indianapolis, IN 46219
317-356-6986
Detroit Publishing Co.
*Barry & Carolyn Yancey
Barry's Postcards
P.O. Box 1865
Anderson, IN 46011
317-643-8455
*Thomas M. Zollinger
1023 Markle Ave.
Elkhart, IN 46517-1620
219-522-3954
Old Cards, Moderns, Supplies

IOWA
Dean Petersen
Dean Petersen Post Cards
4232 Orleans Ave.
Sioux City, IA 51106
712-276-4760, 712-252-1060
General Line
Lois Pietz
Past & Present
435 24th St.
Ames, IA 50010
515-233-1513
Midwest Views, Artist Signed,
Magazines
Pat Ryan
Ryan's Cards
343 26th St. N.W.
Cedar Rapids, IA 52405
319-396-7241
Depots, Topicals, Towns
Wally Searcy
Wapsicard-Iowa Postcard Depot
3240 Whittier Rd.
Springville, IA 52336
319-854-7359
Iowa & Midwest Views, Topicals

KANSAS
*Dan Lambert
P.O. Box 57
Hutchinson, KS 67504
316-669-8664
*Dick & Sue Lightle
P.O. Box 2562
Kansas City, KS 66110
913-334-3186

*Hal Ottaway
Auction Americana
P.O. Box 780282
Wichita, KS 67278-0282
316-686-5574
Kansas & Bordering States, Presidential
Campaigns, Rare & Unusual

KENTUCKY
*Bebe Curry
418 South Elm
Henderson, KY 42420
*Pearl Hess
5117 Mile of Sunshine
Louisville, KY 40219
812-966-2276
*Nancy Lincoln Inn
Nancy Lincoln Lane
Hodgenville, KY 42748
502-358-3845
*Robert Quinn Jr.
P.O. Box 1271
Henderson, KY 42420
502-533-6802
*Stan Walter
1027 Jefferson St.
Paducah, KY 42001
502-442-1740
Worldwide Views, Topicals

LOUISIANA
*Rai Lynne Jarabica
Sanchez's Daughter
P.O. Box 626
Mandeville, LA 70470
504-624-9596
Always Buying, Mail Order,
Appointments, Shows

MAINE
*Lois De Raps
L&L Specialties
38 Military Ave.
Fairfield, ME 04937
207-453-6269
*Alan F. Grab
Grab Bag Antiques, Inc.
39 Main St. (Summer)
Sabattus, ME 04280
207-375-4711
Quality Postcards, Paper Ephemera,
Prints
Bruce D. Nelson
Landmark Postcards
P.O. Box 3565
Portland, ME 04104
207-799-7890
Real Photos, Illustrated Pioneer, Rare &
Unusual
*Robert & Myra Siegel
Salty Professor Antiques
P.O. Box 6202
Cape Elizabeth, ME 04107
207-799-8007
Coney Island, Women, General Line

John Vierra
P.O. Box 6783
Portland, ME 04101
207-657-4399
Mail Order, Show Sales

MARYLAND
*Al Abend
P.O. Box 421
Millington, MD 21651
301-778-1722
*Lee & Shirley Cox
Memory Lane Postcards, Inc.
P.O. Box 66
Keymar, MD 21757
301-775-0188
Shop Sales, Approvals, Auctions,
   Shows
*Roy Cox
P.O. Box 3610
Baltimore, MD 21214
301-483-4778
Book-"How To Price Old Picture
   Postcards"
Catalog-"1992 Specialized Picture
   Postcard Catalog"
*Sheldon Dobres
S. Dobres
P.O. Box 1855
Baltimore, MD 21203-1855
301-486-6569 (eve)
Moderns, Better Pre-1920

*Ward R. Duffey
22 East Ave.
Hagerstown, MD 21740
301-797-8672
*Perry Judelson
P.O. Box 7675
Baltimore, MD 21207
301-655-5239
Views, Topicals, Comprehensive Stock
*Fred H. Lego
6506 Kipling Parkway
Forestville, MD 20747
301-735-6556
*George & Marcella Lorden
522 South Streeper St.
Baltimore, MD 21224
301-675-6098
*Mary L. Martin
Mary L. Martin LTD.
231 Rock Ridge Rd.
Millersville, MD 21108
301-987-7550 (day) 301-647-7975 (eve)
Topicals, U.S. Views, Quality Artists
*James Morrison
P.O. Box 38
Georgetown, MD 21930
301-648-5759
*Wade & Sunny Rice
The Wishbone
P.O. Box 1331
Wheaton, MD 20915

*S&J Collectibles
100 Longridge Ct.
Timonium, MD 21093
301-252-1318
*Fava C. Sherrard
Fava Cards
455 Spring Hill Rd.
Rising Sun, MD 21911
301-658-6359
*Donald E. Wachter
923 Seminole Rd.
Frederick, MD 21701
301-662-1258

MASSACHUSETTS
Noel W. Beyle
P.O. Box 946
North Eastham, MA 02651
508-255-3389
Lifesaving, Ships, Lighthouses
Sally S. Carver
179 South St.
Chestnut Hill, MA 02167
617-469-9175
Early U.S. Expos & Advertising, Better
   Cards, No Approvals
*Donald F. Craig
163 New Boston Rd.
Fall River, MA 02720
508-675-0024

*Harris & Jayne Gray
The Grays
P.O. Box 246
Brookfield, MA 01506
508-867-7210
U.S. Views & Topicals
*Alan R. Lavendier
Whale Deltiology
P.O. Box 40812
New Bedford, MA 02744
508-993-9006
New Bedford Area Views
*Michael O'Brien
35 Bullfinch St.
North Attleboro, MA 02760
Mail Auctions
*Art Ross
P.O. Box 95
Dennis, MA 02638
508-385-5480
*Paul V. Ryan
25 Blackwood Ave.
Billerica, MA 01821
508-667-1103
*Richard Spedding
Richard's Postcards
22 Tanglewood Rd.
Sterling, MA 01564
508-422-8480
Topicals, Views, Approvals
Edward F. Stefanik
P.O. Box 2558
Fall River, MA 02722
617-674-9090
*Ed Valladoa
Valladoa's
P.O. Box 484
84 Rt. 6
Mattapoisett, MA 02739
508-758-3381
Shop Sales
*Gregory Wilson
215 Chestnut St.
Florence, MA 01060
413-586-8554
*Michael Zwerdling
P.O. Box 240
Boston, MA 02130
617-524-7560
Quality Real Photos

MICHIGAN
John & Matt Abbott
Estate Coin & Postcards
725 S. Adams
Birmingham, MI 48009
313-540-0044
*David Jaeger
Dave's New/Used Cards
9114 Warner Rd.
Haslett, MI 48840
517-675-5474
*Ronald D. Millard
Cherryland Postcard Auction Co.
P.O. Box 485
Frankfort, MI 49635
616-352-9758
Postcards, Covers, Mail Auctions

*Laurence & Elizabeth Nordhoff
Trade Winds
336 N. Main St.
P.O. Box 248
Watervliet, MI 49098
616-463-8281
Michigan Views, House of David
*Michael G. Price
M.G. Price
P.O. Box 7071
Ann Arbor, MI 48107
313-668-7388
Foreign Countries, Mail Order
*Judy Ripple
1038 S. Main St.
Apt. F2
Ann Arbor, MI 48104
313-994-5739, 313-764-3167
Pre-1920 Greetings & Topicals
*Doris Waggoner & Kathi Gorske
Postcards from the Attic & Cellar
P.O. Box 145
Williamsburg, MI 49690
616-267-5506
Approvals, Appointment Only
*Martha J. Walton
707 Collegewood Dr.
Ypsilanti, MI 48197
313-482-8354
*Juanita E. White
55 Greble St.
Battle Creek, MI 49017
616-965-0545
Craig Whitford
Numismatic Card Co.
P.O. Box 14225
Lansing, MI 48901
517-483-8374
Coin Cards, Macerated Cards, U.S.
   Mints

MINNESOTA
Fred & Gail Schiffman
Fred & Gail Schiffman Post Cards
2907 Morgan Ave. N.
Minneapolis, MN 55411
612-529-4937
General Line, Moderns
*Mary Twyce
601 E. 5th St.
Winona, MN 55987
507-454-4412

MISSISSIPPI
*Edgar & Georgia Manuel
E&G Postcards
2800 Edgewood Dr.
Meridian, MS 39307-4041
601-483-9658
U.S. States, Greetings, Elvis

MISSOURI
*William W. Burt
5419 Oak
Kansas City, MO 64112
816-444-5414

*Charles M. Moler
K-C's Antiques
110 E. Washington
St. James, MO 65559
314-265-5391
U.S. & Foreign
Stan & Jane Pepper
Pacemaker Auction
3048 Dodridge Ave.
Maryland Hgts., MO 63043
314-291-5972
Approvals

MONTANA
*Frank Houde
Houde's Postcard
Box 2577
Missoula, MT 59806
406-549-2115

NEBRASKA
Bill Cloran
Abraham's Corner
2708 Y St.
Lincoln, NE 68503
402-474-2696
States, Greetings, Real Photos
Robert D. Farley
The Paper Parson
Box 34651
Omaha, NE 68134
402-571-7811
Real Photos, Paper Ephemera
*John & Lynne Farr
P.O. Box 6086
Omaha, NE 68106
402-334-0284
RMS Titanic, Better Topicals,
   Midwestern States
Holmes Publishing
P.O. Box 11
Gothenburg, NE 69138
308-537-3335
Willard Mullin Postcards

NEVADA
*Ervin J. Felix
P.O. Box 3953
N. Las Vegas, NV 89030
702-643-0115
*Tracy Garrett
P.O. Box 18000-52
Las Vegas, NV 89114
702-737-3218
Approvals: Views & Topicals
*Trilby Mary Roman
General Delivery
Gardnerville, NV 89410
702-782-3946

NEW HAMPSHIRE
*Don & Pam Barnes
48 Milbern Ave.
Hampton, NH 03842
603-926-5740

Q. David Bowers
P.O. Box 1224
Wolfeboro, NH 03894
603-569-5095 (weekdays)
Pre-1915 NH Real Photos, Main Streets,
    Commercial Scenes
*James B. Kahn, MD
Route #107
Deerfield, NH 03037
603-463-7105
WWII Propaganda (Germany, Italy,
    Other)
*William J. Pieterse
62 Boston Post Rd.
Amherst, NH 03031
603-673-1945
*Gordon Root
RFD 1 Box 93
Lancaster, NH 03584
603-788-2276
*Chris Russell
Chris Russell & the Halloween Queen
P.O. Box 499,
4 Lawrence St.
Winchester, NH 03470
603-239-8875
Foreign Views, Halloween, Greetings,
    Art Nouveau, Artist Signed

NEW JERSEY
*John E. Bell
1788A Springfield Ave.
New Providence, NJ 07920
201-464-9254
Carlton F. Bloodgood
Carlton's Modern Postcards
P.O. Box 111
Bogota, NJ 07603
Classico, American, Ludlow, Dover
*Saul & Marcia Bolotsky
The Paper Works
63 Columbus Ave.
Lakewood, NJ 08701-3052
908-363-2192
*Barbara J. Booz
The Card Shark
1 Lewis St.
Perth Amboy, NJ 08861
201-442-4234
Northeastern State Views
Shirley Carroll
9 Wagner Lane
Manasquan, NJ 08776
201-223-2276
Frank Chmiel
350 Marc Dr.
Toms River, NJ 08753
201-349-5221
*Daniel B. Duffy
20 Lenox Ave.
Yardville, NJ 08620
609-585-6177
*Sheldon Halper
Cobweb Collectibles
9 Walnut Ave.
Cranford, NJ 07016
908-272-5777
Postcards, Automobile, Toys

*Eleanor & Don Hart
El-Donal Post Cards
41 Preston Ave.
Bridgeton, NJ 08302
609-451-0087
*George C. Hartnet
335 E. Main St.
Moorestown, NJ 08057
609-235-6772
*Fred Herrigel
Box 80R
Oakhurst, NJ 07755
908-775-8997
Pre-1920 Real Photos, Main Streets,
    Store Fronts
*Daniel Herzog
177 Tuxedo Parkway
Newark, NJ 07106
*John J. Kowalak
Camera Retrospect
19 Coles Court
River Edge, NJ 07661
201-487-5721
Custom Printed Real Photos

John McGrath
Jersey Shore Shows
95 Newbury Rd.
Howell, NJ 07731
908-363-3121
New Jersey
*Vin Minner
21 Boulevard Rd.
Cedar Knolls, NJ 07927
201-267-3132
Pre-1950 Topicals & Views, Cigarette &
    Gum Cards
*Richard & Anita Novick
17 Abbey Lane
Marlboro, NJ 07746
201-536-2532

*Don & Newly Preziosi
Preziosi Postcards
P.O. Box 498
Mendham, NJ 07945
201-543-4721
Better Eclectic Older Cards, Top-Notch
    Linens, Contemporary Social/
    Political Issues
*John F. Rhody
686 River Rd.
Fair Haven, NJ 07704
201-758-9436
Herbert & Christine Richardson
Richardson Books
209 Stratford Ave.
Westmont, NJ 08108
609-854-3348
New England & New Jersey Views,
    Farm Buildings, Mills
Mike Schwartz
5 Pasture Rd.
White House Sta., NJ 08889
201-236-9675
*Donald W. Wayne
23 Plymouth Court
Piscataway, NJ 08854
201-463-1527

NEW YORK
*Bernard Aclin
P.O. Box 330
Bronx, NY 10475
212-671-4575
*Edward J. Beiderbecke
P.O. Box 155
4674 Ridge Rd.
Williamson, NY 14589
315-589-2287
Real Photos, New York State Views,
    Railroad Stations
*Thomas J. Boyd
140 Andover Lane
Williamsville, NY 14221
716-626-0089
State Views, World's Fairs, Santas,
    Halloween
*Ken Butts
The Picture Post Card Man
97 Fairhaven Dr.
Cheektowaga, NY 14225
716-634-5970
New York State, Elvis, Trains,
    Airplanes
*Agnes Cavalari
Old Windsor Antiques
R.D. #2, 345 Bethlehem Rd.
New Windsor, NY 12553
914-564-6775
Northeastern States, Glamour
*E & S Antiques
P.O. Box 514
Huntington Station, NY 11746
516-271-5889
*Frank & Hilda Ely
19 North St.
Livonia, NY 14487
716-346-3715
*Wes Finch
P.O. Box 219
Smithville Flats, NY 13481
*Armand J. Florez
P.O. Box 1921
New York, NY 10156
*Nancy Foutz
P.O. Box 459
Rosendale, NY 12472
914-658-3233
Mail Order, Shows
*George C. Gibbs
P.O. Box 614
Syracuse, NY 13201
315-472-0691
Postcard Auctions Specializing in
    Transportation, Political, Rare &
    Unusual
*Marilyn Gottlieb
Marilyn's House of Postcards
P.O. Box 35
Rock Hill, NY 12775
914-796-3244
U.S. Small Towns, Foreign, Topicals
*Al & Norma Hansen
P.O. Box 84
Levittown, NY 11756
516-579-7674

*Paul Harig
Harig's
P.O. Box 2146
Glens Falls, NY 12801
518-792-5523
Mail Bid Sales, Postal History

*John & Betty Henel
79 Fruehauf Ave.
Snyder, NY 14226
716-839-4174
Views, Entertainers, Ships

*Robert E. Juceam
Philatelic Specialties Co.
106 Hemlock Rd.
Manhasset, NY 11030
516-365-7696, FAX 516-365-7697
Stamp Cards, Third Reich, Germany
Printed to Private Order

Joan & Jeff Kay
1816 E. 26th St.
Brooklyn, NY 11229
718-375-7353
5 New York City Boroughs, Long
Island, Advertising, New Jersey

*Dorothy King
355 Finley Rd.
Ballston Spa, NY 12020
518-885-6110

*Bob & Mary Kurey
The Post Card People
585 Overbrook Rd.
Johnson City, NY 13790
607-797-3040
Photo Cards

*S.R. Nelms
P.O. Box 633
Hicksville, NY 11756
516-579-9432
General Line

*Ray Pesarchic
P.O. Box 143
Mayville, NY 14757
716-753-2840

Vincent Peterson, Jr.
928 Dellapenna Dr.
Johnson City, NY 13790
607-797-5723

*Frank J. Pichardo
P.O. Box 1116
Flushing, NY 11354
212-359-1183
World Ocean Liners

*Arlene L. Raskin
2580 Ocean Pkwy.
Apt. 2L
Brooklyn, NY 11235
718-998-1910

*Robert J. & Joan Rau
J & B Postcards
Trackside II
Michael Circle C11
Johnstown, NY 12095
518-736-1163

*Leah Schnall
67-00 192nd St.
Flushing, NY 11365
718-454-1272, 718-454-0582

*Jane Schryver
226 Main St.
Dansville, NY 14437
716-335-3121
Views

Robert Skotarski
Bare Jays Air
35 Cardy Lane
Depew, NY 14043
716-683-2322
Commercial Airplanes, Airports

*Tom & Pat Snyder
P.O. Box 9447
APO, NY 09012

*Hans Tanner
5990 Groveland Hill Rd.
R.D. #2
Geneseo, NY 14454

*Fred Timan
Atlantis Rising Antiques
450 Main St.
Catskill, NY 12414
518-943-7657
Postcards, Paper Ephemera

*Barbara H. Trovei
P.O. Box 317
Port Jervis, NY 12771
914-856-8572

*Nancy Williams
Nancy's Antiques
7217 Lake Ave.
Williamson, NY 14589
315-589-8400
Pre-1920 Postcards, Advertising Trade
Cards, Trade Catalogs

*Florence (Flo) Wit
Flo's Follies
120 Paumanake Ave.
Babylon, NY 11702
516-661-0522, FAX 516-422-3655
Rock & Roll, Pin-Ups, Postcard Shows

NORTH CAROLINA
*Fred N. Kahn
258 Stratford Rd.
Asheville, NC 28804
704-252-6507
U.S. Views, Topicals

*Joe L. Mashburn
Mashburn Cards
P.O. Box 609
Enka, NC 28728
704-667-1427
Artist Signed

*Herbert M. Schulman
P.O. Box 507
Dillsboro, NC 28725
704-586-6572

OHIO
*Barbara Agranoff
P.O. Box 32054
Cincinnati, OH 45206
513-281-5095

*Sam Armao
35887 Mildred St.
N. Ridgeville, OH 44039
216-327-1098

*Ellen H. Budd
6910 Tenderfoot Lane
Cincinnati, OH 45249
513-489-0518
Signed Artists, Topicals, Clapsaddle &
Brundage Books, Approvals, No
City/Town Views

*Jenny Eichinger
Jenny's Antiques
53 N. Main St.
Germantown, OH 45327
513-855-7995
General Line

Rosemary Green
2864 Hastings Rd.
Cuyahoga Falls, OH 44224-3754
216-923-9362
Postcards, Trade Cards, Ephemera

*Clay Griffin
1100 Merriman Rd.
Akron, OH 44303
216-867-7290

R.E. Hartzell
Gene's Cards
2300 Glenway Rd.
Dayton, OH 45404-2127
513-233-6921
General Line, Postmarks, Covers

*Evelyn J. Himebaugh
1703 Wayne Ave.
Dayton, OH 45410
513-256-4625

*Emily & Hank Jamieson
Jamieson's Post Cards & Antiques
1709 Oak St.
Girard, OH 44420
216-545-3963, 412-528-2300
Pennsylvania & Ohio Views

Paul W. Jones
217 N. Prospect St.
Bowling Green, OH 43402
419-352-8657
Ohio, Folders, British Movie Stars

*Paul & Irene Knapp
25028 Rainbow Dr.
Olmsted Falls, OH 44138
216-234-4441

*Keith B. Knight
Mail Pouch Antiques
311 Cass St.
Maumee, OH 43537
419-893-2708
Real Photos, Ohio & Michigan, Great
Lakes Ships, Signed Artists

*Karl Korzeniewski
249 East Baird Ave.
Barberton, OH 44203
216-745-7703

*James T. Lee
P.O. Box 770913
Cleveland, OH 44303
216-671-1725

Jo Long
1437 Mayland Dr.
Cincinnati, OH 45230-2753
513-231-9289
Topicals, Coral-Lee

*John & Sandy Millns
Millns Postcards
40 N. Third St.
Waterville, OH 43566
419-878-0285
Quality Cards, Mail Approvals, No
    Views

Betty Powell
P.O. Box 571
Worthington, OH 43085
Artist Signed, Topicals, Views

*Elliot & Ann Robins
Xenia Antiques
P.O. Box 615
Xenia, OH 45385
513-376-8065

Frank Ryan
111 Norcross Rd.
Zanesville, OH 43701
614-453-9084
Ohio Views, Pre-1925 Topicals, No Mail
    Order

*Don Skillman
6646 Shiloh Rd.
Goshen, OH 45122
513-625-9618

*Hobart & Rosaline Smith
The Smiths
1505 Blanchard Ave.
Findlay, OH 45840
419-422-2154

OKLAHOMA

John & Jean Dunning
J and J Junk
P.O. Box 14033
Oklahoma City, OK 73113
405-840-4035
Buy, Sell, Trade

Don L. Fowler
Box 595A
Canton, OK 73724
405-886-3418
Oklahoma Real Photos

*The Martin House
3216 E. Haskell
Tulsa, OK 74110
918-834-2783

*Doyle & Wanda Payne
P.O. Box 1000
Antlers, OK 74523
405-298-2688

OREGON

*Maxine Cozzetto
2228 N.E. Gilsan
Portland, OR 97232
503-232-4656

*Jocelyn Howells & Edouard Pecourt
Jocelyn Postcards
P.O. Box 22223
Portland, OR 97222
503-658-6437
Quality Cards

*Doug Walberg
Glimpse of Time
Route 1, Box 428
Bandon, OR 97411
503-347-3881
Real Photos, Photographs

Shirley M. Wilson & Harry M. Kelsey
Rainbow's End Book Co.
250 Broadalbin St. S.W.
Albany, OR 97321
503-926-3867
Pre-1920 Oregon & Washington,
    General Line

PENNSYLVANIA

*Paul & Sandra Anna
Anna's Postcards & Collectables
102 Woodlawn Ave., Apt. E-18
Horsham, PA 19044
814-956-9788
Views, Topicals

*Col. J.R. Ballow
P.O. Box 88
Camp Hill, PA 17011

*Henry V. Betz
294 Briar Lane
Chambersburg, PA 17201
717-263-3165

*Gladys Bruce
23 Green Meadow Circle (Summer)
R.D. #5
Ephrata, PA 17522

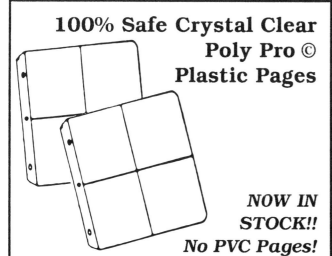

*Robert H. Shaub
350 W. Railroad Ave.
Shrewsbury, PA 17361
717-235-3309

*Alan E. Stricker
The Nickel Trader
3025 Washington Rd.
McMurray, PA 15317
412-941-2338
Approvals

*Sy Trabin
15 High Rd.
Levittown, PA 19056
215-945-3194

*George Trach
Box 67
Rillton, PA 15678
412-446-7627
General Line

*Treasure Chest
P.O. Box 187
Covington, PA 16917
717-659-5413

Jim Ward
P.O. Box 300
Lititz, PA 17543-0300
Lancaster City & County, Fire Engines

Fred W. Zaiser
210 E. Walnut St.
Sellersville, PA 18960
215-257-1686
Topicals, Views, No Real Photo

Evan & Fran Zlock
198 N. Chancellor St.
Newtown, PA 18940
215-968-7650

SOUTH CAROLINA
*Myrta W. Hall
P.O. Box 657
Lane, SC 29564
803-387-6062

*Jim Petit
P.O. 4097
N. Myrtle Beach, SC 29597-4097
803-272-3802
All Eras, Topical, Geographical

TENNESSEE
*V. Ray Foster
1302 Arno Rd.
Franklin, TN 37064
615-794-7124

*Joe & Marian Frye
P.O. Box 111301
Memphis, TN 38111
901-458-3911

TEXAS
Agnes Barnes
3533 Basque
Waco, TX 76710
817-776-1783
1950-1970 Chromes, 1930 Real Photos
     (France, Mexico)

*Glenn J. Butler
P.O. Box 28757
Dallas, TX 75228
214-327-0626
Texas, Transportation, Better Cards

Irmabeth Dittmer
Penney's Postcards
619 Thistlewood Dr.
Houston, TX 77079
713-497-4780

Bob & Kathy Fesler
Fesler's Auctions
3802 Caney Creek Rd.
Austin, TX 78732
Mail Auctions, Buying Collections

*Laurence Gretsky
1507 Edgewood Ave.
Austin, TX 78722
512-476-7063

*James McMillin
Mac's Used Cards
3306 Ave. "D"
Fort Worth, TX 76105
817-535-3961

*William & Patricia Petersen
322 Scott St. (Winter)
San Marcos, TX 78666
512-353-7574

*Ruth Scott
1615 Bluebonnet Dr.
Fort Worth, TX 76111
817-834-0103
General Line

UTAH

Goreham Collectibles
1539 East 4070 South
Salt Lake City, UT 84124
801-227-5119

VERMONT

*Jack Hamelle
Shepard's Pie In The Sky
50 Canada St.
Swanton, VT 05488
802-868-2264
Topicals, New England States, New York

*Clint Studwell
P.O. Box 1298
Hardwick, VT 05843

VIRGINIA

*Jeff Bradfield
Jeff's Antiques
745 Hillview Dr.
Dayton, VA 22821
703-879-9961
Virginia Views, General Line

*Ken & Darlene Cochran
P.O. Box 309
Crimora, VA 24431
703-249-5507

*Marge Davis & Chuck Evans
118 Brown Bark Pl.
Ashland, VA 23005
804-798-4214

*Gayle Floyd
Gayle Floyd, Inc.
8107 Greeley Blvd.
Springfield, VA 22152
703-569-9566
Washington D.C., Greeting Cards, Hand-Colored French Romantic Cards

*Dr. & Mrs. Bob Gardner
Dr. Nostalgia
3237 Downing Dr.
Lynchburg, VA 24503
Topicals, State Views

*Bob Karrer
P.O. Box 6094
Alexandria, VA 22306
703-360-5105
Panama Canal Zone, Rep. of Panama

*John McClintock
P.O. Box 1765
Manassas, VA 22110
703-368-2757

*Sylvia Regelson
Ouroboros
Antique Village
U.S. 301
Richmond, VA 23111
804-353-8397, 804-730-8004
General Line, Better Artists

*Mary Jayne Rowe
Mary Jayne's Railroad Specialties, Inc.
Route 5, Box 132-A
Covington, VA 24426
703-962-6698
Modern Transportation Postcards

*Kitty Smith
404 Rugby CT.
Falmouth, VA 22405

*Vintage Images
P.O. Box 3140
McLean, VA 22103
703-642-5394

*John Whiting
Whiting's Old Paper
P.O. Box 25058
Richmond, VA 23260
804-746-4710
General Line

WASHINGTON

*Mike Fairley
Fairlook Antiques
81-1/2 S. Washington
Seattle, WA 98104
206-622-5130, 206-364-9997
Postcards, Photos, Ephemera

*Joan Klepac
The Ultimate Pet
28828 207th Ave. S.E.
Kent, WA 98042
206-630-2012
Dogs, Horses, Approvals

*Walter Lozoski
910 4th Ave. North
Seattle, WA 98109
206-285-4986
Washington Real Photos

*Michael Maslan
Michael Maslan Historic Photos,
    Postcards & Ephemera
P.O. Box 20639
1216 3rd Ave.
Seattle, WA 98102
206-587-0187
Real Photos, Ephemera, Photographs

*Richard & Myra McDonald
R&M International
P.O. Box 6278
Bellevue, WA 98008-0278
206-865-8104
Auctions, Shows, Approvals

John F. McNamara
Columbia View Cards
Rt. 1, Box 512
Long Beach, WA 98631
206-642-3398
Modern Western Views, Covered
    Bridges

Mary E. Patterson
A.J. Smith & Co.
110 Alaskan Way South
Seattle, WA 98104
206-624-9104
Postcards, Victorian Scrap, Trade Cards

*Burton E. Pendleton Sr.
Vintage Postcards
E. 2130 Sprague Ave.
Spokane, WA 99202
509-535-4368
Pre-1930, Photographica

*Kent & Sandra Renshaw
Potlatch Traders
P.O. Box 574
Freeland, WA 98249
206-321-0729
High Quality Postcards, No Mail Sales

Virgil Reynolds
P.O. Box 194
Walla Walla, WA 99362
509-525-6410
Topicals, States

Robert Ward
Antique Paper Guild
P.O. Box 5742
Bellevue, WA 98006
206-643-5701
Mail Auctions for Pre-1935 Real Photos

WEST VIRGINIA

*Richard Bain
P.O. Box 2
Colliers, WV 26035
304-527-1724

*Curtis & Ruth Duckett
P.O. Box 674
Rainelle, WV 25962-0674
304-438-7659
Pre-1920 & Real Photo State Views,
    Topicals, Real Photos

WISCONSIN

Richard Furchtenicht
P.O. Box 4041
Madison, WI 53711
608-274-1901

Rolland Gundlach
914 S. Gammon Rd.
Madison, WI 53719
608-271-6653

Roger L. Haag
Haag's Coins
Box 211
Sun Prairie, WI 53590
608-837-8042
Quality Real Photos, General Line,
    Views

Lois Heft
1305 Debra Lane
Madison, WI 53704
608-241-0851

Terry Kempf
1302 Ruttedge St.
Madison, WI 53703
608-255-6205

Sharon Lake
51 S. Bowman Rd.
Wis. Dells, WI 53965
608-253-7861

Frank Lindemann
1313 Dakota St.
Watertown, WI 53094
414-261-0666

Willa Severson
2438 E. Mifflin St.
Madison, WI 53704
608-244-3759

*Joe Stransky
P.O. Box 1672
Madison, WI 53701
U.S. Views, Postmarks, Foreign Views

WYOMING

*George & Evelyn Herman
Pack Rat Antiques
P.O. Box 2287
Cody, WY 82414

CANADA

*John De La Vergne
RR2, Cooks Mills Rd.
North Bay, ONT P1B 8G3
705-472-8577

Larry Garfinkel
Garfinkel Publications
Box 46617, Sta. G
Vancouver, BC V6R 4G8
604-736-6912
NW Coast Indians, Cut-out Postcards

*Neil Hayne
P.O. Box 220, 147 Church St.
Bath ONT K0H 1G0
613-352-7456
Topicals, Worldwide Views, Paper
    Canadiana

*Donald Kaye
D. & L. Kaye Enterprises
P.O. Box 4201, Sta. D
Hamilton ONT L8V 4L6
416-957-7227
Canada, Postal History, Britain

*Quality Stamps & Covers Inc.
P.O. Box 296
St. Albert, ALB T8N 1N3
403-460-2540
Transportation, USA Real Photo,
    Foreign

Michael J. Swiech
Silver Maple Stamps
P.O. Box 89
Denwood, ALB T0B 1B0
403-842-2873
Waterloo Co. Ontario, Military

*Catherine M. Wright
George S. Wegg, LTD.
53 Adelaide St. East
Toronto, ONT M5C 1K6
416-363-1596
Canada, Foreign, Topicals

DEALERS
Don't Be Left Out in '92!

Send your information to: *Postcard Collector Annual*, P.O. Box 337, Iola, WI 54945

Postcard Collector
Index

This index to *Postcard Collector* provides a variety of listings that should prove valuable to researchers interested in learning more about the hobby of deltiology and specific cards, artists, etc. The index includes all issues from the magazine's beginning in November 1983 through December 1990. It will be updated yearly. Photocopies of specific references are available from *Postcard Collector* at a cost of 50 cents per page. Requests for photocopies should be directed to the Editor, *Postcard Collector*, P.O. Box 337, Iola, WI 54945.

PRINTERS INDEX

PUBLISHERS & DISTRIBUTORS INDEX

Postcard Show Calendar Listing

Postcard Clubs: Clip or copy this form.
Use it to announce your postcard shows in the
1992 Postcard Collector Annual.

DATE (month, days) _____

LOCATION (state, city) _____

SHOW NAME _____

LOCATION (site, street address, directions) _____

_____

_____

TIME (specific hours each day) _____

ADMISSION _____ # OF POSTCARD DEALERS_____

CONTACT PERSON (name, address, telephone) _____

_____

_____

Mail to: *Postcard Collector Annual,* Show Calendar Listing,
P.O. Box 337, Iola, WI 54945.

GET 12 ISSUES OF POSTCARD COLLECTOR FOR ONLY $19.95

Postcard Collector is the hobby's leading, most informative postcard publication!

Each monthly issue is packed with tips and ideas from experts on how to buy, sell, display, preserve and enjoy your postcards. You'll stay on top of the newest releases and the latest finds. Plus you'll find thousands of postcards for sale in the hobby's largest, most widely-read marketplace!

HERE'S WHAT INFORMED COLLECTORS ARE SAYING ABOUT
Postcard Collector!

"I enjoy your magazine *Postcard Collector* very much! Very informative, lots of photos, auctions and a wide range of advertisers. Surely there's something for everyone."

Harold Barkley,
Barkley Museum, Taylor, MO

"I collect modern and older cards. Everyone has different tastes and your magazine is good for telling about all of them. Thank you for giving me something to look forward to each month."

Alison Jones,
Malta, OH

Visa, MasterCard, Am Ex Orders, Please call TOLL FREE

1-800-331-0038

_____ Start or
_____ renew my subscription to:

POSTCARD COLLECTOR

_____	1 Year	(12 issues)	$19.95
_____	2 Years	(24 issues)	36.50
_____	3 Years	(36 issues)	52.50
		(Your best buy)	

Foreign addresses, please send the following amount which includes additional postage and handling charges: 1 yr - $29.95; 2 yrs - $55.00; 3 yrs - $80.00.

Please provide payment in the form of a U.S. funds check drawn on a U.S., Canadian, or Mexican bank.

Name _____

Address _____

City _____

State _____ **Zip** _____

Credit Card # _____

Expires: Mo _____ **Year** _____

Signature _____

Clip this coupon and mail with payment to:

Postcard Collector
P.O. Box 337, Iola WI 54945   Annual